In these troublesome times I
of the blessed hope of God's
cise manner Doc defines th
to theology, documents how
theologians throughout history, and shows from Scripture
how God used it to save the righteous from His judgments.
Based on the signs around us, Doc concludes the next rapture will be the last one—and that is welcome news indeed.

—DEREK GILBERT
SKYWATCHTV

From Enoch to Elijah to the end days of the church, Doc
takes you through a historical ride through time using
both biblical and historical evidence that brings very com-
pelling pre-tribulation information to the great rapture
debate! This book makes you long for that great and glorious day of the return of our redeemer, Lord, and Savior
Yeshua/Jesus Christ.

—DAN BIDONDI
INFOWARS REPORTER
RADIO TALK SHOW HOST OF THE *DAN BIDONDI SHOW*
AND *TRUTH RADIO SHOW*

As a prophecy teacher and lecturer, Doc Marquis has intu-
itive knowledge of the Scriptures and the prophecies in
the Book of Revelation. His knowledge of the Scriptures
will give the reader timely and prophetic insight of the last
days we are about to experience.

—PAUL WALTER
CEO AND SENIOR EDITOR OF NEWSWITHVIEWS.COM

the Marquis reminds readers
final rapture. In a clean coll
the word rapture as it applies
has been used by Christian

THE
FINAL
RAPTURE

THE
FINAL
RAPTURE

DOC MARQUIS

FRONT
LINE

Most CHARISMA HOUSE BOOK GROUP products are available at special quantity discounts for bulk purchase for sales promotions, premiums, fund-raising, and educational needs. For details, write Charisma House Book Group, 600 Rinehart Road, Lake Mary, Florida 32746, or telephone (407) 333-0600.

THE FINAL RAPTURE by Doc Marquis
Published by FrontLine
Charisma Media/Charisma House Book Group
600 Rinehart Road
Lake Mary, Florida 32746
www.charismahouse.com

Unless otherwise noted, all Scripture quotations are taken from the Modern English Version. Copyright © 2014 by Military Bible Association. Used by permission. All rights reserved.

Scripture quotations marked KJV are from the King James Version of the Bible.

Cover design by Vincent Pirozzi
Design Director: Justin Evans

Visit the author's website at
www.itsagodthingproductions777.com.

Library of Congress Cataloging-in-Publication Data:
Names: Marquis, Doc, author.
Title: The final rapture / Doc Marquis.
Description: Lake Mary, Florida : FrontLine, [2017] | Includes
   bibliographical references.
Identifiers: LCCN 2017029352| ISBN 9781629991832 (trade
paper) | ISBN
   9781629991849 (ebook)
Subjects: LCSH: End of the world. | Rapture (Christian
eschatology)
Classification: LCC BT877 .M28 2017 | DDC 236/.9--dc23
LC record available at https://lccn.loc.gov/2017029352

17 18 19 20 21—9 8 7 6 5 4 3 2 1
Printed in the United States of America

DEDICATION

No CHRISTIAN CAN take full credit for what he understands as a child of God. All of us are a collection of things we learned through the Bible, at church, at Sunday school, at Christian colleges and universities, and so on. And like every other born-again Christian, I am the product of those things I learned along my Christian path. However, there is one major source that kept me anchored and very well grounded in my understanding of the Word of God. This particular source gave me a sure foundation with a cornerstone that is immovable. That single source, my educational sure foundation, is known as Louisiana Baptist University (LBU), my alma mater (class of '84), and it is this educational institution to which I proudly dedicate this book.

My professors—Dr. Jimmy Tharpe (founder of LBU), Dr. Edith Tharpe, Dr. Ray J. Norton, Danny Dodson, "Meemaw," and others—taught me many aspects of Christianity that I use to this very day. They opened my eyes to the Word of God, they enriched my life as a Christian, and each of them in their own way enabled me to have a better walk with the Lord. There is no possible way I could ever repay them for all they taught me, but at least I can say thank you for their investment in me. Each of them is part of who and what I am today.

I was only two years old in the Lord when I first stepped into Louisiana Baptist University and met a number of Christian brothers and sisters whom I shall remember until the good Lord calls me home: Jeff, who taught me that Christians have steely resolve; Al, who taught me how to have patience in the Lord; Rodney, who taught me how to have a childlike wonder of the Lord; Brenda, who taught me how to laugh at everything, especially the enemy when he is causing me trouble; Sherry, who taught me how to have tolerance through the power of God; and last but certainly not least, Gerald, who taught me commitment to the Lord. This book, *The Final Rapture*, is also dedicated to each of them.

CONTENTS

Part I:
Which Rapture Are We Waiting For?
(The Past)

Part II:
How Close Are We?
(The Present)

Part III:
Hope for the Unsaved
(The Future)

ACKNOWLEDGMENTS

NO PERSON WRITES a book by himself anymore. It takes a dedicated team to make a writer's dream come true, turning him from a simple writer into a published author. At Charisma House I had a wonderful team that made my dream come true: Maureen Eha, Megan Turner, Kimberly Overcast, Stephanie Arena, Leigh DeVore, and Joshua Dorlon.

I would also like to thank those ministries, Christian publications, and radio and television programs that have helped me make it this far: Prophecy Watchers, Cutting Edge Ministries, Southwest Prophecy Ministries, News With Views, *The Hagmann and Hagmann Report* with Doug and Joe Hagmann, *Radio Liberty* with Dr. Stan Monteith, *Raiders News Network* with Dr. Tom Horn, *Time Out With Kevin Gallagher*, *Prophecy in the News* with Dr. Kevin Clarkson, *Apocalypse and the End Times* with Paul McGuire, and *Pass the Salt Live!* with Coach Dave Daubenmire.

And especially to the Most High Jesus Christ, King of kings and Lord of lords, who explained to me more than thirty years ago what a rapture is truly all about.

FOREWORD

WHAT DAYS WE are living in! Our world now is nearer to the brink of nuclear war than ever—rogue nations getting closer to acquiring nuclear weapons, smoldering tensions with China and North Korea, the ever-present "Israel problem" in the Middle East, and the Islamic immigration and makeover of Europe. Divisions over politics and ideology foment violence, protests, riots, and ugly civil debates in the United States.

New advances in technology now seek to "download" human consciousness into computers, merge human brain cells with biochips and data receivers, extend human life and fighting abilities through genetic manipulation with other species, and preserve the body beyond death by freezing it for "reanimation" when the capability is developed.

Interest and direct involvement in the occult is exploding in America and around the globe, both through pop culture and personal participation in dark pagan rituals. Fascinatingly, as Western civilization turns its back on its Christian roots, entering a so-called post-Christian era, we are presently poised to regress back into a new "Dark Ages."

With all these unsettling developments, our world seems to be rushing headlong toward a new world order.

And this fearful climate has precipitated a more keen and heightened awareness and interest in biblical prophecy. Many are discovering for the first time or rediscovering anew those ancient Hebrew and Christian holy writings predicting how the present age climaxes and closes.

Into what was for centuries a clean, tight interpretation of these end-time scenarios, controversy has entered in the last several years. Most of it has centered around the timing of the resurrection and retrieval of Christians, or what we commonly call the rapture. When I first heard the author of this book present these truths in person at a prophecy conference I was hosting, as he spoke he was loudly and very rudely interrupted by a most disrespectful brother who shouted, "Be not deceived!" The man was asked to leave the room of several hundred people.

Turn to any website discussing things prophetic and read the thread of comments. It almost always blows up into an argument over when the rapture will occur: before the time of awful tribulation, at the halfway point, or more nearly three-fourths of the way through that period. Defenders of each position seem passionate and vociferous, sometimes even snarky.

Into this theological fray enters our brother and friend Doc Marquis. The book you hold distills his four decades of ministry and biblical study into a most lively and readable presentation of the truth of Scripture about the rapture of the saints. Doc's unique experience of salvation from an occult background makes his perspective even more pertinent. The Bible says the last days will be a time of lying signs and wonders, false prophets, and a resurgence of ancient pagan religions.

The Final Rapture answers the questions of controversy

in unique fashion. With good historical survey, linguistic analysis, solid scriptural appeal, and firm logic, we are presented with the early church's belief about the catching up of the saints. Not stopping there, the book goes on to discuss the major signs of the times that the Bible predicted, and we can see happening in our world today.

The last section of *The Final Rapture* is a heartfelt witness and message to those people who will be left on Earth after the rapture occurs, telling how to be saved and providing a bird's-eye flyover of the contents of the Book of Revelation. Doc Marquis has handled this material in superb, easily understood fashion. I hope you will enjoy it as much as I did!

—Dr. Kevin Clarkson
Host, *Prophecy in the News*
Pastor, Oklahoma City

INTRODUCTION

WHY WRITE THIS book? With so many books out there on the eschatological teachings of the rapture, why did I choose to add to the count? Surely the topic of the rapture has been all played out by now.

Several months ago I was asked to speak at a major prophecy conference and, as always, I attempted to teach as much as I could in the one hour that had been allotted me. After the presentation I had more than fifty people come up to me and ask me over and over again: "Where did you come up with this teaching? Why aren't we being taught this from behind the pulpit? Our pastor has never preached about this." And by the time I made it back to my table, the one hundred copies of the DVD titled *Which Rapture Are We Waiting For?* were gone—and it had been less than an hour. I was gobsmacked, to say the least.

A couple months later I was approached by Joshua Dorlon of Charisma House and asked to write a book on the rapture. Charisma House expressed comments similar to those of conference attendees who heard my teachings on the rapture. I've been told these teachings are unique, that no one has seen anything like this before, and that everyone should learn about these teachings. I take no credit for these teachings; these are things God taught me over the years. I am simply a messenger, a teacher trying to educate my brothers and sisters. Lord willing, I'll do a good job of it. But these teachings I taught at the conference are just part 1 of this book. And those teachings deal with the past.

In part 2 we take a hard look at the present. We do this because there are what I call "pre-signs" that need to be carefully examined. Most who have looked into eschatology have learned of the major signs that precede the next and final rapture. However, there are pre-signs, other events that are to happen before the major signs that signal the rapture. And it's by examining these pre-signs that we garner a much better understanding of just how close we truly are to the next and final rapture.

In part 3 of this book we turn our attention to the future. You and I will already be in heaven once the rapture has occurred, but what about those who have to live through the Tribulation? What happens to them? Over the last thirty-eight years, years in which by the grace of God I have been a born-again Christian, I have pondered the fate of those who would have to endure the Tribulation. What can we do for them? Surely there must be a way to reach out to those unsaved people in the future. And that's what part 3 does; we shall reach out to those in the future and try to get them saved. "How?" you ask. We will be in heaven and these individuals will be on the earth during the Tribulation. We won't be able to reach anyone then. So how do we reach out to them?

We set up a timeline of events that will occur according to the Book of Revelation. Step by step we will go through the major prophetic events so that everyone in the future will know what to expect. By doing so, we will not only prove the accuracy of the Word of God, but we also will prove the Word of God has been right all along, which will bring as many as possible to salvation. In essence, we are sending them a letter in a bottle. That letter is about what they can expect to happen during the Tribulation and that they need to be saved while there's still time because the Tribulation is only seven years long and after that comes the Final Judgment. Lord willing, we and 144,000 Jewish evangelists who will be unleashed on the earth will be able to bring even more to salvation through this message. I pray that even though we are living in the present, we can still make a difference for those in the future. And why couldn't we? After all, we do serve God, who always has been, always is, and always will be. He is God over everything, including time. God bless and keep each of you out there.

Part I
WHICH RAPTURE ARE WE WAITING FOR?
(THE PAST)

Chapter 1
THE DEFINITION OF *RAPTURE*
AND ITS HISTORICAL USAGES

T HE RAPTURE IS one of the simplest concepts found in the Holy Bible. It was so basic a point that the apostles, who walked with our risen Lord and Savior, didn't even bother to make it a doctrine. Nor should it be a doctrine! It is only when we add our own opinions and perspectives that the rapture becomes a confusing issue.

Before we begin looking at Scripture and the pre-tribulation rapture of the church, let me point out that God has never punished the righteous with the unrighteous. Tear through Scripture if you will and try to find just one righteous person who was punished along with the unrighteous. You will be wasting your time, because no such event has ever occurred. And when we apply a little bit of common sense, we know it wouldn't make sense for such a thing to occur. Who would want to worship a God who would unjustifiably punish a righteous person with unrighteous people who have earned such punishments?

In beginning to look at a pre-tribulation rapture, it is important to know that believers are not appointed to face the wrath of God. By definition, an appointment is a time and a place someone is supposed to be for something to happen. One very quick and easy example is a doctor's appointment. That appointment commits you to be at a certain place at a certain time to see the doctor.

First Thessalonians 5:9 reads: "For God has not appointed us to wrath..." In other words, we are not designated to have a time or a place where we will have to face the wrath of God. There will be times when God will punish us for something we've done, but facing the whole of God's wrath is something else.

Why aren't we appointed to face the wrath of God? What makes us (born-again Christians) so special that we get to avoid God's wrath? The answer is found in John 3:36: "He who believes in the Son has eternal life. He who does not believe the Son shall not see life, but the wrath of God remains on him."

Because we are saved, we do not face the wrath of God, nor do we have an appointment to face His wrath. Those who are not saved not only have the wrath of God abiding on them, but many also "drink of the wine of the wrath of God" (Rev. 14:10). Scripture also tells us that "the wrath of God" is going to be poured out "on the earth" (Rev. 16:1; see vv. 1–17). Since the Bible already clearly pointed out that we are not appointed to wrath, then we cannot be present during the Tribulation since His wrath is going to be poured out on the whole Earth. It's that straightforward; it's that clear-cut. We do not have an appointment to face the wrath of God, which means we cannot be here during the Tribulation. This all works together to prove that there will be a pre-tribulation rapture.

Only when we begin to mix in our opinions and our perspectives does the rapture, which is so straightforward, become unclear. Quite frankly, if God wanted our opinion, He would've asked for it!

THE DEFINITION OF
THE WORD *RAPTURE*

The word *rapture* is derived from the Greek word *harpazo*. This word, *harpazo*, has many meanings, but each is similar. This word is used seventeen times in thirteen verses in the Greek New Testament. As you can see below, it is used in a number of different ways, yet each holds a very similar definition:[1]

1. In Matthew 13:19 and John 10:12 the word *catcheth* (KJV) is used for the Greek word *harpazo*, which in those two cases means "carry off."

2. In Matthew 11:12 *harpazo* is used twice and translated as "take" and "by force" (KJV). This occurs once again with the same words, "take" and "by force" (KJV), in John 6:15.

3. In Acts 23:10, where *harpazo* is used twice within the phrase *take him by force* (KJV), *harpazo* is first defined as "to take" and then defined as "forcibly."

4. In John 10:28–29 the word *pluck* (KJV) is translated from the Greek word *harpazo*, which in those two verses means "to take."

5. In Jude 23 the word *pulling* (KJV) is used for the Greek word *harpazo*, which means to lead away.

6. In Acts 8:39 the words *caught away* (KJV) are from the Greek word *harpazo*, which means "carried away."

7. In 2 Corinthians 12:2 and 4, 1 Thessalonians 4:17, and Revelation 12:5 *harpazo* is translated as "caught up" (KJV), which means "caught up." (That was an easy one to translate.)

I'm sure by now you can easily see that the Greek word *harpazo* is translated into English with several different words. However, the definition revolves around the same meaning: something or someone that is being physically removed or relocated. This is the essence of the word *harpazo*, and it is applicable to each example in those thirteen verses. We will use the words *physically removed* as our general definition for the word *rapture*. If we were to try to use all the various different words for rapture, such as *catch up, take by force, catch away, pluck, catch, pull, to seize, carry off by force, to snatch out, to snatch away*, and so forth, we would all be crazy by the time we were finished with this chapter. Suffice it to say we will use the general term *physically removed* for our study.

Before moving on any further, allow me to explain that in our normal, everyday conversation we never use the word *harpazo* unless we're having a conversation in Greek. Instead we use the word *rapture*. Through a process of transliteration, which means translating the spelling of a word from one language into another language, *rapture* came from *harpazo*:

- *Harpazo* is a Greek word, which when transliterated into Latin becomes *rapio.*

- *Rapio* is a Latin word, which when transliterated into English becomes *rapture.*

- *Rapture* is an English word.

All three words—*harpazo, rapio,* and *rapture*—have the same meaning. They just have their origins in different languages. And that's it! The meaning remains unchanged.

Is the Rapture a Modern Idea?

There are those people who will say (and I've heard this one plenty of times over the decades) that the word *rapture* doesn't appear in the Bible. First of all, the word *Bible* doesn't appear in the Bible, yet I still know I'm reading a Bible. So that excuse is foolish at best.

The word *rapio,* which as mentioned above is from where we derive the English word *rapture,* is found in 1 Thessalonians 4:17 of the Jerome Bible, also known as the Vulgate, which was a Latin translation of the Bible.

Another group of people out there have told me that the word *rapture* has only recently been used and applied in any biblical sense, such as claims that the church is going to be raptured before the Tribulation.

Many say the rapture is a new concept because of an event that happened less than two hundred years ago. Back in 1830 a fifteen-year-old girl of Irish-Scottish descent named Margaret MacDonald had a vision of a post-tribulation rapture. Notice carefully, her vision depicted a post-tribulation rapture and not a pre-tribulation rapture. She said:

> This is the fiery trial which is to try us. It will be for
> the purging and purifying of the real members of
> the body of Jesus.... The trial of the church is from
> Antichrist. It is by being filled with the Spirit that
> we shall be kept.[2]

Notice carefully how Margaret stated that this fiery trial (the Tribulation) is meant to test the real members of the body of Jesus. And note especially that Margaret tells us this testing comes from the Antichrist. Well, no matter which perspective you come from, this so-called trying of the members of the body of Jesus could only happen during or shortly after the Tribulation begins and *not* before it. In other words, Margaret MacDonald's so-called vision was *not* a vision of a pre-tribulation rapture. Yet many people, including false apostles and false teachers, won't tell you that. All they usually say is that the teachings of the rapture of the church began with Margaret MacDonald. Many purposely leave that her vision was a post-tribulation perspective and not a pre-tribulation perspective.

It is from the vision of Margaret MacDonald that John Nelson Darby in the nineteenth century supposedly used the word *rapture* to describe what Margaret had seen once he had heard of her vision. This would mean that the word *rapture* (as a biblical application) originated less than two hundred years ago and no sooner. That is utter nonsense! This argument that the rapture is a new idea is one of the things that really ruffles my feathers because those who make this argument are lying, either knowingly or unknowingly. They might not have an understanding of literary applications of the word *rapture*, or maybe they are lying even with this knowledge because they have some sort of personal agenda. Whatever the case, the rapture is not a new idea.

HISTORICAL USES OF
THE WORD *RAPTURE*

To show the nonsense of the idea that the rapture is a new concept, I'm going to show you that the biblical applications for the rapture are much older than John Nelson Darby or Margaret MacDonald. I'm going to start in the twentieth century and work all the way back to the fourth century.

The following is only a partial list of literary works that contain a biblical application of the word *rapture*. I used some examples after MacDonald and Darby to show that the true understanding and application of the word *rapture* was not changed by those events but was still cherished and held on to despite how hard Satan tried to destroy it.

- 1909—*Scofield Reference Bible*[3]

- 1878—*Jesus Is Coming* by W. E. Blackstone[4]

- 1866—*Hereward the Wake* by Charles Kingsley[5]

- 1748—*An Exposition of the New Testament* by John Gill[6]

- 1667—"Paradise Lost" by John Milton[7]

- 1610—*A Display of Heraldrie* by John Guillim[8]

- 1526—*The Pylgrimage of Perfection* by William Bonde[9]

- ca. 1342—*Polychronicon* by Ranulphus Higden[10]

- 1412–1420—*Chronicle of Troy* by John Lydgate[11]

- ca. 1400—*The Vernon Manuscript*[12]

- 405—The Vulgate (Latin translation of the Bible)[13]

Rapture has been spelled a number of ways in English over the centuries because of linguistic evolution. As languages change, so does the spelling of certain words, as in the case of the word *rapture*:

- The ancient Latin is *rapio* or *rapere* and other such usages

- In the early English period (1066–1154) what we now know as *rapture* was spelled *rapt*

There is nothing more to it than that! It is simply a matter of linguistic evolution or change.

Now that we have examined the translation of the word *rapture* and its historical significance and applications, let's move on to our next chapter and delve into the literary evidence for the rapture.

Chapter 2
THE HISTORICAL CONCEPT OF
THE PRE-TRIBULATION RAPTURE

T HE LIE (EITHER stated knowingly or unknowingly) that the pre-tribulation rapture of the church is a new concept that can only be traced back to 1830 and Margaret MacDonald's vision is simply that—a lie! I will now present another literary list that proves once and for all that the pre-tribulation rapture of the church is not a new concept but a teaching that came directly from the apostles themselves. This list will begin before 1830 and go all the way back to the first century. The works of any of the authors below would be accepted by any court in the land as physical evidence of the teaching of the pre-tribulation rapture, a perspective that was taught for almost two millennia before Margaret MacDonald.

- Thomas Scott—In his first collection of sermons published in 1796, he taught that the righteous will be carried to heaven, where they will be secure until the time of the judgment is over.[1]

- James Macknight—In *A Harmony of the Four Gospels*, originally published in 1763, he taught that the righteous will be carried to heaven until the judgment is finished.[2]

- John Gill—In the 1748 An *Exposition of the New Testament* he taught of the imminent return of Christ, first at the rapture and then again to judge the earth (the second coming of Christ during Armageddon).[3]

- Morgan Edwards—He was one of the original trustees of what is now Brown University and wrote of his pre-tribulation rapture beliefs in 1744.[4]

- Philip Doddridge—In *The Family Expositor*, originally published in 1739, he taught a pre-tribulation rapture perspective.[5]

- Peter Jurieu—In *The Accomplishment of the Scripture Prophecies* (1687) he wrote that Christ would return during the rapture, take His saints to heaven, and later return at the Battle of Armageddon (the second coming).[6]

- Ephraem the Syrian—He preached of a pre-tribulation rapture ca. 373.[7]

- Victorinus—Sometime around 300 he wrote of the church being "taken away."[8]

- Cyprian—Cyprian lived from 200–258. He wrote of a pre-tribulation rapture in *Treatises of Cyprian*.[9]

- Irenaeus—In *Against Heresies* he wrote of the church being suddenly caught up. Irenaeus lived from 130–202.[10]

- Ignatius of Antioch—Ignatius was a student of the apostle John and lived ca. 36–108.[11] He also wrote of the pre-tribulation rapture.[12]

- Clement of Rome—Clement lived in the first century. His first letter to the Corinthians implies a pre-tribulation rapture of the church.[13]

I personally challenge those of the mid-tribulation perspective or post-tribulation perspective to come up with a literary list, such as the one just presented, that will demonstrate their belief.

The view of the pre-tribulation rapture of the church, which is the oldest of all the biblical perspectives, could not be stopped. It originated with the apostles of Jesus Christ during the first century, was taught to their students, and continues on to this very day. The mid-tribulation and post-tribulation teachings (which are grossly false) are the new teachings and not the original teaching of Jesus Christ, nor of His chosen apostles or their students. Those are teachings and creations of man and not God.

Now, let's move on to those events that we understand to be raptures.

Chapter 3
BIBLICAL EXAMPLES
OF RAPTURES

PART OF THE scientific method, to paraphrase, teaches us that if the same results happen over and over again under the same conditions, then it (whatever it is) is a fact. By applying the scientific method, we're going to try to determine if there is a biblical pattern for the pre-tribulation rapture.

Before we do that, let me ask you this: What makes a rapture a rapture? That probably seems like a silly question to some people, but think about it for a moment. When I asked this question of my brothers and sisters in the past, 99 percent of them told me a rapture is "when Christ is coming back in the clouds to take us away." They answered the question in that way because they did not consider what I was asking. I asked "What is *a* rapture?" not "What is the *next* rapture?" You see, my dear brothers and sisters, there have been many raptures in the past, as you will shortly find out.

WHAT CONSTITUTES
A RAPTURE?

An event requires only three simple details to be considered a rapture:

1. God physically removes people.

2. He removes those He declares to be righteous.

3. He takes them outside of His impending judgment.

There is only one exception to this rule that I know of, but we'll get to that one later on. For now, remember a rapture is when (1) God physically removes (2) those He declares to be righteous (3) outside of His impending judgment. This is a pattern found throughout the Bible. There have been numerous raptures in the past that have followed this exact same pattern.

Before anyone starts to jump out of their skin, hear this matter all the way through. Remember, Scripture says, "He who answers a matter before he hears it, it is folly and shame to him" (Prov. 18:13). Now let's look for that biblical pattern for the pre-tribulation rapture of the church.

NOAH AND THE ARK

In Genesis 6 we find out that man's wickedness was great and that every thought of theirs was evil (Gen. 6:5). Because of this, God was going to destroy His own creation (Gen. 6:7). However, God instructed Noah to build an ark where his family would be kept safe from the impending flood (Gen. 6:14–16).

Was this a rapture? This is a big question, but the answer is clear: it most certainly was a rapture. Let's apply the three principles of a rapture and see how they fit in:

1. Did God physically remove them? Yes, Noah and his family were removed from their home and placed on the ark (Gen. 7:7).

2. Did God declare them righteous? Yes, Genesis 7:1 tells us that Noah and his household were righteous before God.

3. Were they taken outside of God's impending judgment? Yes, Genesis 7:23 shows us the end result of God's judgment upon His creation. Only Noah and his family, the ones God declared righteous, survived.

Beyond any shadow of a doubt, the events surrounding Noah and the Flood constitute a pre-tribulation rapture. Noah and his family were removed *before* God's judgment hit the earth and not during or after. Are there any other examples of such raptures? Of course there are. Let's move on to the next one.

LOT AND THE CITIES OF SODOM AND GOMORRAH

In Genesis 18 we read that three men (or angels, one of whom some believe was Jesus Christ) paid Abraham a visit. After it was revealed that Sarah would bear a son even though she was well beyond the ability to conceive a child, the three men rose up and looked toward Sodom (Gen. 18:10, 16). When it was revealed that the three men intended to destroy Sodom and Gomorrah for their unbounded sins, Abraham tried to intervene (Gen. 18:20–23).

Abraham asked a very revealing question that is

extremely pertinent to the rapture. To me, it reads as if Abraham was absolutely horrified about what could happen. Once it was revealed that those cities were about to be destroyed, Abraham asked, "Shall You also destroy the righteous with the wicked?" (Gen. 18:23). This concept seemed almost outside of Abraham's ability to comprehend, as it should have been! Remember, God doesn't punish the righteous with the unrighteous (wicked). This is why Abraham was so afraid of what might have happened. Genesis 18:25 tells us that according to Abraham's understanding, God just doesn't work like that. Abraham said, "Far be it from You to do such a thing as this, to slay the righteous with the wicked." In other words, "You don't judge people like that. The righteous are different from the wicked and do not deserve to be punished."

To further his cause, Abraham petitioned the Lord not to destroy Sodom if righteous people were found in it (Gen. 18:24–32). The exchange between the two is below:

- Abraham asked if God would destroy Sodom if there were fifty righteous people (Gen. 18:24).

- The Lord said He wouldn't touch the place if there were fifty righteous people (Gen. 18:26).

- Abraham asked if God would destroy Sodom if there were forty-five righteous people (Gen. 18:28).

- The Lord said He wouldn't touch the place if there were forty-five righteous people (Gen. 18:28).

- Abraham asked if God would destroy Sodom if there were forty righteous people (Gen. 18:29).

- The Lord said He wouldn't touch the place if there were forty righteous people (Gen. 18:29).

- Abraham asked if God would destroy Sodom if there were thirty righteous people (Gen. 18:30).

- The Lord said He wouldn't touch the place if there were thirty righteous people (Gen. 18:30).

- Abraham asked if God would destroy Sodom if there were twenty righteous people (Gen. 18:31).

- The Lord said He wouldn't touch the place if there were twenty righteous people (Gen. 18:31).

- Abraham asked if God would destroy Sodom if there were ten righteous people (Gen. 18:32).

- The Lord said He wouldn't touch the place if there were ten righteous people (Gen. 18:32).

There was only one righteous man, Lot, in the city of Sodom. As Genesis 19 records, two of the angels went to Sodom, met Lot, and told him what they were about to do. The angels instructed Lot to find his sons-in-law, sons, daughters, and such, and take them out of the city (Gen. 19:12). It was night by this point, and Lot had only until the morning to warn his relatives and get them out. Unfortunately no one listened. As Genesis 19:15 records, when the morning came, the angels basically told Lot to move it because judgment was about to hit Sodom.

Lot lingered, and the angels, knowing that God's wrath was about to be unleashed, grabbed Lot and his family by the hands and almost dragged them out of the place. Lot and his family were instructed to flee to the mountains and not to look back upon Sodom as it was being destroyed (Gen. 19:16–17). We find out in verses 24–25 that Sodom, Gomorrah, all the inhabitants, and the entire area were completely wiped out!

Lot told the angels that he did not want to escape to the mountains because he was afraid something would happen to them along the way (Gen. 19:19). He suggested that instead of sending them to the mountains, the angels should send them to the small city of Zoar, and the angels accepted Lot's suggestion (Gen. 19:20–22). The response from the angels reveals a lot if we read it carefully. To paraphrase their response, the angels stated that they would allow Lot and his family to go to Zoar, and even though it was originally going to be overthrown, it would not be overthrown now because Lot would be living there (Gen. 19:21).

So why wasn't Sodom overthrown before Lot left? And why was Zoar not overthrown since that had been the plan? It is simple—Lot lived in Sodom and was moving to Zoar. Lot's presence prevented both cities from being touched.

What is the connection? What was so special about Lot that wherever he lived remained untouched by God's just judgment? Lot was righteous! Second Peter 2:7–8 tells us that Lot was a "righteous man." Let's not forget that the angel (the Lord) revealed to Abraham that Sodom would not be touched if righteous people were found in it.

Do the events that happened in Sodom constitute another rapture? Again, yes!

1. Did God physically remove them? Yes, God physically removed Lot and his family (Gen. 19:16).

2. Did God declare them righteous? Yes, God considered Lot righteous (2 Pet. 2:7–8).

3. Were they taken outside of God's impending judgment? Yes, Sodom and Gomorrah and the surrounding area experienced God's judgment, but Lot and his family were safe outside of this area (Gen. 19:24–25).

Once again we have another rapture! All the elements necessary for a rapture are found in the events surrounding the destruction of Sodom and Gomorrah.

MOSES AND THE TEN PLAGUES OF EGYPT

The events leading to the destruction of Sodom and Gomorrah revealed to us that because righteousness (Lot) was found in Sodom, God would not judge the place until that righteousness (Lot) had been removed. Only after the righteous man Lot had been "raptured" out of Sodom could God then punish it. Plus, the city of Zoar, which appeared to have been on the list of cities about to be destroyed, was spared destruction because "righteous" Lot was going to move into that place. The angelic messengers gave us a critical piece of information pertaining to what constitutes a rapture. In short: those who are righteous must first be removed before God will punish a place with His judgment.

In the story surrounding the events of Moses's confrontation with Pharaoh, we are going to see another snippet of information that will further our understanding of what makes a rapture a rapture.

When Moses met God at the burning bush, he was given orders to free the Israelites, who had been living in an occult, polytheistic society for 430 years, most of the time as slaves (Exod. 1:8–14; 3:3–10; 12:41). The rod Moses was carrying was blessed with divine power, and Moses went with his brother, Aaron, to deliver God's message to Pharaoh (Exod. 4:2–5; 5:1).

In Exodus 7:7 we learn that Moses was eighty years old and Aaron was eighty-three when they began to confront Pharaoh. Once they confronted Pharaoh with the first three signs—the rod turning into a serpent (Exod. 7:10), the waters turning to blood (Exod. 7:20), and the frogs coming out of the waters and covering the land (Exod. 8:6)—something very vital was revealed that is extremely important to our study of the pre-tribulation rapture.

Moses was instructed by God to tell Pharaoh to let His people go or He would send swarms of flies throughout Egypt (Exod. 8:20–23). It's in verse 22 that we find out something very important—God said He would "in that day set apart the land of Goshen, in which My people dwell, so that no swarms of flies shall be there." The land of Goshen is in the northernmost section of Egypt. It was given to Joseph and his family by Pharaoh, and it was the best of the land of Egypt (Gen. 47:6). But a new king turned all of the Israelites into slaves and kept them as such in Goshen (Exod. 1:8–14).

So God separated the land of Goshen from the rest of Egypt. To further emphasize His point, God instructed Moses to tell Pharaoh that He would "put a division between My people and your people" (Exod. 8:23). God made it abundantly clear that He had separated not only His people (the Israelites) from the Egyptians but also the land in which they lived (Goshen). In other words, God physically removed the Israelites to the land of Goshen. And it's this separation, or physical removal, that is the first part of what constitutes a rapture.

The second part of what makes a rapture a rapture is that there has to be a declaration of righteousness. Did God ever declare as righteous the Israelites who were held captive in Egypt? Yes! In Romans 4:11 we find out that the Israelites had a seal of righteousness upon them through Abraham; the "sign of circumcision, a seal of the righteousness of faith" began with Abraham and continued as a sign for all of Israel. This righteousness was imputed, or credited, to them. Circumcision was a physical (outward) sign of their faith in God. When you read Romans 4:11–13 carefully, you'll discover that the seal of righteousness given to the Israelites was both a physical and a spiritual sign. So because the Israelites had righteousness as a seal upon them, they fulfilled the second part of what constitutes a rapture.

The third part of a rapture, when people are taken outside of God's judgment, is described beginning in

Exodus 8:22. God Himself stated that "no swarms of flies shall be [in Goshen]." During the next plague the livestock, horses, donkeys, camels, oxen, and sheep of Egypt were stricken with a "grievous pestilence" or "murrain" (Exod. 9:3–6), which was possibly a form of what we now call anthrax.[1] Yet verse 6 indicates that this pestilence did not touch the livestock of the Israelites. God did not physically touch even the cattle of the Israelites. Why? Because during a rapture, there is a division, a separation. Just as had already occurred with the plague of flies, the children of Israel were outside of God's judgment. The account of the plagues of Egypt also indicates that the boils of the sixth plague were upon the magicians and the Egyptians (but not the Israelites); the hail of the seventh plague was everywhere in Egypt except Goshen; the locusts of the eighth plague were intended for the houses of Pharaoh, his servants, and the Egyptians; the Israelites "had light in their dwellings" during the ninth plague, darkness; and the Lord passed over the houses of the Israelites during the final plague of the death of the firstborn (Exod. 9:11, 25–26; 10:5–6, 23; 12:12–13, 29–30). The children of Israel remained outside of God's judgment throughout the plagues.

Do the events that happened during the ten plagues of Egypt constitute another rapture? Yes!

- Did God physically remove them? Yes, the Israelites were set apart in the land of Goshen.

- Did God declare them righteous? Yes, the Israelites had the seal of righteousness upon them.

- Were they taken outside of God's impending judgment? Yes, the Israelites were not subjected to the plagues of Egypt.

Once again all the elements of a pre-tribulation rapture are in place. And this time God even told us in His own words part of what constitutes a rapture: there is a division, a separation, or a setting apart of the people who are declared righteous from the unrighteous (or wicked) outside of His impending judgment.

We will be looking at other raptures later in this book, but for now let's move on to the final rapture, the next rapture that will occur.

THE NEXT RAPTURE

The final rapture that will happen is described in 1 Thessalonians 4:16–18:

> For the Lord Himself will descend from heaven with a shout, with the voice of the archangel, and with the trumpet call of God. And the dead in Christ will rise first. Then we who are alive and remain shall be caught up together with them in the clouds to meet the Lord in the air. And so we shall be forever with the Lord. Therefore comfort one another with these words.

The Bible also teaches us about the final rapture in 1 Corinthians 15:51–53:

> Listen, I tell you a mystery: We shall not all sleep, but we shall all be changed. In a moment, in the twinkling of an eye, at the last trumpet, for the

trumpet will sound, the dead will be raised incorruptible, and we shall be changed. For this corruptible will put on incorruption, and this mortal will put on immortality.

There are other verses in the Bible that add to our understanding of the final rapture, but what we need to consider now is this: Does the final rapture fit the scriptural pattern of what constitutes a rapture? The answer is yes, it does. And trust me, brothers and sisters, I could write a book on this topic alone, but that would deprive you of the pleasure of doing the rest of the homework yourself.

Before we continue, there are two things I'd like to quickly cover. First, there are those who refer to this final rapture as the "secret rapture." Mind you, they use this term in a condescending manner because of their views and opinions. Such terminology is ridiculous and ludicrous because we know it's going to happen, therefore it cannot be a secret. And when it does happen, it's not as if anyone is going to miss it!

The second thing I want to quickly cover is that the final rapture is not the second coming of Christ! The reason the final rapture is not the second coming of Christ is because He will not physically touch the earth. The first coming of Christ was when He physically walked among us on the earth during the thirty-three years of His life. The true second coming of Christ will be when He physically arrives on the earth again toward the end of the Battle of Armageddon and stand on the Mount of Olives, which will be split in two (Zech. 14:4). During the final rapture the Lord will meet us in the air, not physically on the earth. There's nothing more to it than that. Let's move on!

Does the final rapture contain the three elements necessary to constitute another rapture that is based on the biblical pattern that has been established up to this point? It certainly does.

- Will God physically remove us? First Thessalonians 4:17 proves that we will be "caught up [*harpazo*] together with them in the clouds." It will be a physical removal.

- Has God declared us righteous? Romans 3:22 says, "This righteousness of God comes through faith in Jesus Christ to all and upon all who believe." Christ imbued us with His righteousness when we became saved. (See Romans 5; 8.)

- Will we be taken outside of God's impending judgment? First Thessalonians 5:9 states that we do not have an appointment to face the wrath of God. The seven-year Tribulation as described in the Scriptures will definitely be a time of the wrath of God.

  » "They said to the mountains and rocks, 'Fall on us, and hide us from the face of Him who sits on the throne, and from the wrath of the Lamb, for the great day of His wrath has come'" (Rev. 6:16–17).

  » "The nations were angry, and Your wrath has come, and the time has come for the dead to be judged" (Rev. 11:18).

» "If anyone worships the beast and his image and receives his mark on his forehead or on his hand, he also shall drink of the wine of the wrath of God" (Rev. 14:9–10).

» "The angel thrust his sickle into the earth and gathered the vintage of the earth, and threw it into the great winepress of the wrath of God" (Rev. 14:19).

» "I saw another great and marvelous sign in heaven: seven angels having the seven last plagues, for in them the wrath of God is complete.... Then one of the four living creatures gave to the seven angels seven golden bowls full of the wrath of God.... Then I heard a loud voice from the temple saying to the seven angels, 'Go, pour out the bowls of the wrath of God on the earth'" (Rev. 15:1, 7; 16:1).

» "Babylon the Great was remembered before God, to give to her the cup of the wine of the fierceness of His wrath" (Rev. 16:19).

» "[Christ] treads the winepress of the fury and wrath of God the Almighty" (Rev. 19:15).

Let's face it. God is furious! However, God be praised, we will not have to face His wrath because we are saved, and we will not be on the earth during the Tribulation. And one other thing to especially note is that this final rapture was compared to the ones that happened during the Flood of Noah (Matt. 24:37–42; Luke 17:26–27) and the destruction of the cities of Sodom and Gomorrah (Luke 17:28–29). God thoroughly destroyed His entire creation during the Flood because He was sick and tired of the earth being so sinful (except for the righteous family of Noah), and He also destroyed the cities of Sodom and Gomorrah and the surrounding plains (except for righteous Lot).

What is particularly interesting is that God destroyed the earth with water during the Flood but promised He would never judge His creation like that ever again, and He established the rainbow as proof of His covenant with His creation (Gen. 9:12–17). God destroyed Sodom, Gomorrah, and the surrounding plains with fire. When we study the Book of Revelation, we find the world will slowly be destroyed by fire. That is one of the main reasons why the next rapture and the outpouring of the wrath of God are being compared and contrasted with Noah and Lot. God's wrath will be poured out upon the unrighteous as it was in the days of Noah and Lot. Since He promised not to destroy the world with water, He will do it with fire after the final rapture as He did with Sodom and Gomorrah. Fire is a purifying element, and the whole earth will be purified of all the sin that was committed upon it.

In the timeline of events described in the Book of Revelation, the next and final rapture is believed to occur at Revelation 4:1. There are good reasons for this:

- Revelation 3:20–22 (right before Revelation 4:1) states that Christ is standing at the door and knocking. This is the Bridegroom

(Christ) seeking the bride (the saints) and not a verse of salvation as many believe it to be. Immediately after this event, the church vanishes.

- From Revelation 4:1 to Revelation 19:13 (the entire Tribulation period) the church is not seen again on the earth. Only after the second coming of Christ at the Battle of Armageddon is the church seen again. Revelation 19:14 refers to the armies of heaven (the church) following Christ as He returns. We will come down at this point and join those who were saved during the Tribulation.

Since Revelation shows us that the church is not seen on the earth until the second coming of Christ, the next rapture fits in perfectly with the rapture pattern of the Bible, where the righteous are removed before the judgment of God occurs. Let's move on.

ENOCH AND ELIJAH

We find out in Genesis 5:21–24 that when Enoch was 365 years old, he was taken by God, and I believe it was to heaven. In verse 24 the word *took* in Hebrew is *laqach*, which means "to be removed." [2] As with all the other examples of raptures, Enoch's removal was a necessary element. In other words, Enoch was physically removed because it is one of the elements that constitute a rapture. We also know that Enoch was righteous. Genesis 5:24 says he "walked with God," and Hebrews 11:5 tells us Enoch "had this commendation, that he pleased God." Now please hold these thoughts for a minute.

From the Book of 2 Kings we find out that "the LORD was about to take Elijah up to heaven by a whirlwind" and that "a chariot of fire and horses of fire separated [Elijah and Elisha], and Elijah went up by a whirlwind into heaven" (2:1, 11). The Hebrew word for take once again is *laqach*, which means "to remove." As with any other rapture, Elijah was physically removed. We also know that Elijah was righteous as he was a prophet of the Lord and "did according to the word of the LORD" (1 Kings 17:5).

Yet there is a problem with the examples of Enoch and Elijah. They met two of the three requirements for a rapture: they were both physically removed, and the Bible shows they were righteous. But where is the third element? Were they removed outside of God's impending judgment?

The Hebrew word *laqach* can also mean "to reserve." [3] Both Enoch and Elijah were removed and taken up to God (as one could expect in a rapture), but there was no impending judgment. The reason this element wasn't necessary was Enoch and Elijah were being reserved for another purpose. And I do mean *reserved*, because neither of them died. There was no death mentioned at all. On the surface this appears to be contrary to Hebrews 9:27: "As it is appointed for men to die once." All of us have an appointment (a time and a place) to die; there are no exceptions. So how does this fit with what happened to Enoch and Elijah?

In Revelation 11:3–12 we discover that two witnesses will prophesy for three and a half years. At the end of three and a half years they will be killed by Satan, but after three and a half days they will be resurrected and then raptured into heaven.

I am convinced the two witnesses are Enoch and Elijah because both witnesses will appear out of nowhere, die, and then be raptured. Enoch and Elijah never died; however, the two witnesses in the Book of Revelation will die in fulfillment of Hebrews 9:27.

There are those who believe that the two witnesses will be Moses and Elijah because the two witnesses will be able to perform miracles:

- Fire will come out of their mouths to destroy their enemies.

- They will be able to stop the rain from coming.

- They will be able to turn water into blood.

- They will be able to cause plagues to occur.

It is true that Elijah stopped rain from coming and called down fire from heaven when he faced the prophets of Baal (1 Kings 17:1; 18:36–38), and while Moses was the mouthpiece of the Lord during the ten plagues, it was mostly Aaron who wielded his rod to make the plagues occur.

When we consider the debate about whether Moses will be one of the two witnesses because they can turn water into blood and cause plagues, Moses simply doesn't add up. It was Aaron, not Moses, who stretched out his rod and turned water into blood. It was Aaron's actions that brought about the plagues of frogs and lice. When considering the criteria of the ability to turn water into blood and cause plagues, Aaron is as likely a candidate as Moses.

Another important point to make is that Moses died a physical death. We find in Jude 23 that the archangel Michael was contending with Satan over the body of Moses. This is verified in Deuteronomy 34:5-7, which states that Moses died at 120 years old in the land of Moab. Since everyone including Moses dies once (Heb. 9:27), I personally believe this excludes Moses from being one of the two witnesses. Why? The two witnesses will die during the Tribulation and will be raptured into heaven after three and a half days.

So you can understand why I don't believe Moses will be one of the two witnesses because he just doesn't fit the description. I will end this section by saying I respectfully choose to disagree with those who believe Moses will be one of the two witnesses based on what I just presented. Whether the two witnesses will be Elijah and Enoch, Moses and Elijah, or perhaps two unknown individuals, no one can say for certain. All we can really do at this point is wait and see.

PHILIP AND
THE ETHIOPIAN EUNUCH

Acts 8:26-40 tells us an Ethiopian eunuch was in his chariot reading a passage from the Book of Isaiah (Isaiah 53:7-8, to be precise) when the Holy Spirit instructed Philip to speak with the Ethiopian, who in the end became saved. After Philip baptized the Ethiopian, "the Spirit of the Lord took [harpazo] Philip away." Philip was later found preaching in Azotus and all the cities along the way unto Caesarea. Philip was physically removed because he was righteous (he was saved), but as was the case with Enoch and Elijah, there was no impending judgment of God about to hit.

It appears that when only one person is raptured (before the final rapture, which will be a global event), only two of the three elements are necessary: physical removal and righteousness. However, whenever there is more than one person being raptured, all three elements are necessary: physical removal, the persons involved must be righteous, and they must be removed from God's impending judgment. In the almost thirty years that I have been teaching this, I have not found any exceptions.

THE LAST TRUMPET

First Corinthians 15:52 tells us that a trumpet is going to be blown that heralds the last rapture. First Thessalonians 4:16–17 also references the trumpet of God in connection with the final rapture. Once the trumpet of God sounds, the rapture occurs.

In Revelation 8:6 we find out that seven trumpets will be given to seven angels. There are those who believe that the final rapture will happen when the seventh trumpet is sounded (Rev. 11:15), which is the mid-tribulation rapture perspective. But there is a problem with that line of thought.

Let me ask a very simple question: What is the purpose behind a trumpet being blown? It's a very simple answer. Unless you are musically inclined, a trumpet is blown to announce the beginning or the end of something, usually an event. This practice goes on to this very day in nations throughout the world. Just think of England for a minute. Whenever the queen opens Parliament, trumpets are blown. After the queen reads her speech, trumpets are once again blown as she exits. And let's not forget that the shofar (a ram's horn used for ceremonial purposes in the Jewish tradition) is blown in order to signal the beginning or the ending of some event.

You cannot say that the last trumpet will be blown during the middle of the Tribulation because the Tribulation period isn't over yet. That kind of reasoning doesn't fit in with why a trumpet is blown. So what's the answer then?

Revelation 3:20 describes the church age coming to a conclusion. Christ is announcing His arrival as the Bridegroom meeting His bride (the church—you and me). The ending of the church age will be announced by the last trumpet as described in 1 Thessalonians 4:16 and 1 Corinthians 15:52. The last trumpet Paul wrote about is the trumpet that will mark the end of the church era. It's that plain, that straightforward, ladies and gentlemen. When you understand the purpose behind a trumpet, it's easy to understand why the last trumpet will be sounded during the final rapture, because it will mark the end of the church age. And when you add in the fact that God has never punished the righteous with the unrighteous, it all becomes very clear.

Those of the mid-tribulation perspective use Daniel 7:25 to support their argument, saying that God will not rescue His saints until the middle of the seventieth week of Daniel: "[The saints] shall be given into his hand until a time and times and half a time." However, we must remember God has never allowed the righteous to be punished with the unrighteous. Also, people will become saved throughout the Tribulation and will later on be martyred (beheaded) because they refuse to worship the Antichrist or take his mark (Rev. 20:4). The Antichrist will assume his full power at the start of the second half of the Tribulation, referred to as the Great Tribulation, and martyr (murder) all those who refuse to worship him. The martyrdom begins during the second half of the Tribulation and not before. So there can be no mid-tribulation rapture because Christians are being martyred after the midpoint of the Tribulation.

One last thing to consider, which is critical to understand, is that the trumpet of God mentioned in 1 Corinthians 15:52 and 1 Thessalonians 4:16 is mentioned nowhere else in the Bible. Why will the trumpet of God be present at this final rapture, and why will it be blown? Because a trumpet is blown for the opening or closing of an event. The event that is being closed is the church age. The history of the church age as found in Revelation 2 and 3 will come to an end, signified by the sounding of the trumpet of God. At that point a new age will begin that will last for only seven years. That age will be the age of Satan. Once it concludes, the Battle of Armageddon will begin. After Jesus Christ's victory over Satan, another new age will begin—the millennial reign of Jesus Christ.

Let me close part 1 of this book by saying that a definitive pattern has been proven to exist in the Scriptures pertaining to the pre-tribulation rapture perspective:

- Multiple examples have been given that satisfy the scientific method, demonstrating that a fact is only proven through repetition with the same outcome.

- With the cases of more than one person being involved, pre-tribulation rapture was the only method ever used; everyone involved was removed before the wrath of God hit, not during or after.

- The three elements that constitute a rapture were met in every case when more than one person was involved.

- Never once in any of the raptures did God allow the righteous to be punished with the unrighteous.

- Scripture clearly teaches that no one who has been declared righteous has an appointment to face the wrath of God or will be punished with the unrighteous.

Those who hold to the mid-tribulation or post-tribulation perspectives cannot show a definitive scriptural pattern as you were just shown with the pre-tribulation rapture perspective. The mid-tribulation and post-tribulation folks will throw a bunch of scriptures at you, so many at times that you can no longer tell heads from tails—and by doing so they easily confuse the issue. Anyone can do that! But they cannot show you multiple events that form a pattern that is based on their perspectives. The only definitive pattern based on multiple scriptural examples and events is the pre-tribulation rapture perspective.

There you have it! The pre-tribulation rapture of the church is the only perspective that lines up with the Scriptures and makes perfect scriptural sense.

Part II
HOW CLOSE ARE WE?
(THE PRESENT)

Chapter 4
THE PROPHETIC MARKER

SOMETHING IS GOING on in the prophetic realm, something you can sense. It's almost as if prophetic ripples are gently flowing through the cosmos, trying to get our attention. It's almost tangible. Personally I've been sensing this prophetic ripple for over five years, and I'm convinced it has to do with biblical prophecy directly related to the next rapture, which I feel will soon occur. And the one question for those who can sense this change coming is, how close are we?

So how close are we, ladies and gentlemen, to the next rapture? That is a tough question to answer but not an impossible one. Before going on, let me point out a very important fact. According to the Bible, "Concerning that day and hour no one knows, not even the angels of heaven, but My Father only" (Matt. 24:36). This verse tells us that no man knows the exact moment when the next rapture shall hit—only God knows. So if anyone tries to tell you the time or the date, call him a liar and a false prophet because God's Word tells us that only He knows when He will send His Son to gather up His children at the next rapture.

We have already examined the timing of the next rapture, which will be a pre-tribulation rapture as with all previous ones. Having said that, we need to find a prophetic marker—a place in the prophetic timeline where we can begin to understand what is going on in the prophetic realm. I feel the best place we can begin our trek is Israel.

THE IMPOSSIBLE NATION

Israel is what I call the Impossible Nation. By any secular standard the State of Israel should not exist. Let's turn our attention to the history of Israel in order to understand why this will be our starting point.

Around 1000 BC King David ruled over the united kingdom of Israel and its capital, Jerusalem, areas that included what is now Israel and the West Bank. King Solomon took over the kingdom when his father, King David, died. In 931 BC, when King Solomon died, the kingdom was divided into two separate parts, Judah in the south and Israel in the north.[1]

A little more than two centuries later, around 722 BC, the Northern Kingdom of Israel was attacked by the Assyrians, who exiled the ten tribes of Israel to other parts of their empire.[2] The Assyrians were invaders from the northern part of Mesopotamia, what is now northern Iraq. Once the invasion was complete, the kingdom of Israel was no more.

Over one hundred years later, after Assyria had fallen, Jerusalem was conquered in 587 BC by the Babylonians under the rule of Nebuchadnezzar II. Many Jews were deported to Babylon, which is modern-day Iraq. The First Temple, built by Solomon, was destroyed.[3]

By 539 BC King Cyrus of Persia (modern-day Iran) conquered the Babylonian Empire.[4] King Cyrus permitted the Jewish exiles to return to Jerusalem and proclaimed that they should "build the house of the LORD God of Israel" (Ezra 1:2–4). Once the Jewish people settled back in their homeland, they rebuilt the Temple of Solomon, or what is also known as the Second Temple.

Then around 331 BC Alexander the Great, who ruled over the ancient world's most vast empire, utterly defeated the Persian Empire and thus became the ruler over Jerusalem and the land of Israel. The Jewish people became part of the Greek Empire.[5]

After the death of Alexander the Great, the Greek Empire was divided into four parts with one of Alexander's generals ruling over each division. The Jews ended up caught in the power struggle between the Ptolemaic and Seleucid empires. Around 168 BC a group of Jews known as the Maccabees revolted against the Greek Empire because Antiochus IV desecrated the Temple.[6] Then in 142 BC the Jews gained their independence when Antiochus IV's successor agreed to their demand. For around eighty years Israel, now known as Judea, was once again independent.[7]

In 63 BC the Romans, under the rule of Pompey, conquered Jerusalem. Although the Jewish people were permitted to continue their religious practices, they were ruled by the Roman Empire.[8] In 37 BC Judea became a province of Rome under the rule of Herod the Great, who was appointed by the Roman Senate.[9] When Herod the Great died in 4 BC, his son Herod Antipas became the ruler of Galilee.[10] This is the same Herod Antipas of the Holy Scriptures.

AD 30

Now let's move the timeline back to AD 30. For most of the past seven and a half centuries the Jewish people were exiled, enslaved, dispersed, invaded, conquered, and finally put under the rule of Herod Antipas, a puppet administrator of the Roman Empire. The history of the Jewish people has been a dismal one.

Jewish history was taken off course. The history of the Jews should have been one of absolute glory, the likes of which the world has never seen. But what caused the history of the Jewish people to become derailed? Where did it all go wrong?

It's really quite an easy answer. The Jewish people asked for it. Originally the Jewish people were under a theocracy—ruled directly by God. But no, they decided they wanted to be like everyone else and have a king. They shot themselves in the foot when they decided to do things their way and not God's way. And the rest, as they say, is history.

By the year AD 30 Jewish history had been tumultuous at best. But there was one thing at least that still solidified the Jews as a people: the Second Temple.

The Second Temple was one of the most incredible structures throughout the entire region. Its massive outer walls were thick and ran around the entire Temple Mount. Nowadays we can only guess at what its original splendor and glory must have been like.

Now imagine for a moment that a man and twelve friends went into the Second Temple. The man looks at all of it, turns around, and declares, "Truly I say to you, not one stone shall be left here upon another that shall not be thrown down" (Matt. 24:2). Obviously we're speaking of Jesus Christ.

Imagine overhearing that conversation—that this magnificent center of worship, this glorious Second Temple, is going to be destroyed. Considering the history of the

Jewish people, the prospect of having the Second Temple destroyed would have been horrifying.

AD 70

Four decades later, after tolerating one Jewish uprising after another, Emperor Vespasian sent his eldest son, Titus, to take care of the Jewish uprisings once and for all. Titus was a renowned war leader and hero in the eyes of the Romans. And if he was given a situation to deal with, militarily speaking, he would deal with it.

In AD 69 the armies of Titus surrounded Jerusalem and laid siege to the city. They cut off all the outside food and water supplies. By AD 70 Titus and his armies had broken through the outer walls and attacked. According to the ancient historian Josephus, when Titus and his armies entered Jerusalem, they killed more than one million Jews. Almost one hundred thousand more were captured and enslaved. The Temple was destroyed.[11]

Titus was crowned emperor of Rome in AD 79, nine years after he destroyed the Second Temple and took Jerusalem. One of his greatest achievements as emperor was the completion of the famous Colosseum in Rome.[12] Many historians believe that the great Colosseum was built by Jewish slaves, more than likely the captured Jews from Jerusalem.[13]

The destruction of the Second Temple was foretold by Christ four decades before it happened. We need to take note at this point that Christ foretold that not one stone of the Second Temple would be left upon another, that all of the stones would be thrown down. In other words, the entire structure of the Second Temple would be brought down.

There is controversy among historians about whether Titus's intent was to destroy the Second Temple. The famous first-century historian Josephus claimed that the destruction of the Second Temple began when a Roman soldier, despite orders from Titus to the contrary, threw a torch inside its walls that started a fire, which was considered a normal or expected method of warfare.[14] Others state that it was always Titus's intention to raze the Second Temple to the ground.[15] One thing is certain: all the stones that were a part of the Second Temple were quite literally pulled apart and the destruction of the Second Temple was complete.[16]

I believe there is more merit in the belief that Titus intended to destroy the Second Temple all along, based upon a story an old friend of mine told me ages ago. Back in the mid-1980s I knew a historian who had traveled extensively throughout the Middle East all of his life. He told me a story he learned from the native people, who told him that the Second Temple was purposely destroyed and why.

There was an old myth, a legend if you will, in those early days that stated that the legendary wealth of King Solomon and the Temple treasures had not vanished as history taught. According to the legend, Solomon's wealth and the Temple treasures were melted down and covered by the mortar used to cement the Temple stones together. Titus had heard of this legend when he besieged Jerusalem, and once his armies destroyed the city, he ordered that every stone of the Second Temple be pulled apart. Titus believed that all of Solomon's gold could be found in between those huge stone blocks. However, nothing was ever found. Nevertheless, as Christ foretold, all of the stones of the Second Temple were pulled apart and thrown down. And for the most part, Israel as a nation was destroyed, and the remnants of the Jewish people eventually were scattered throughout the world.

It appeared that the State of Israel would end up as a distant memory, a footnote in the annals of history. However, another prophecy the Lord had given would come into play. But that prophecy would not be fulfilled for almost two thousand years.

THE FIG TREE

For more than 1,800 years Israel was a memory, a byword, a nation of the ancient world that had its moment in the sun but had come and gone. As with all the other nations that over the course of history disappeared and whose people were dispersed and absorbed into other cultures, no one would have expected Israel to reemerge as an independent nation. Yet the Scriptures clearly indicate that Israel is part of God's master plan, and Israel's reemergence as a nation was prophesied long before it occurred.

In the parable of the fig tree, the Lord said, "Now learn a parable of the fig tree: When her branch is yet tender and puts outs leaves, you know that summer is near. So also, when you see these things come to pass, know that it is near, even at the doors. Truly I say to you, this generation will not pass away until all these things happen" (Mark 13:28–30). Mainstream Christian theology teaches us that the fig tree represents Israel and that the budding of its leaves refers directly to the return of Israel as a nation. However, because Israel originally rejected Christ as the prophesied Messiah, the return of Israel as a nation was going to be accompanied by heavy birth pains.

Ottoman Rule
and Zionism

Beginning in the sixteenth century the Ottoman Empire ruled Palestine after they conquered the entire Middle East.[17] During that time there continued to be a Jewish presence in that part of the world, especially in the holy cities of Jerusalem, Safed, Tiberias, and Hebron.[18]

In the early 1880s there were approximately twenty-five thousand Jewish people living in Palestine. However, due to the persecution of Jewish people in Europe toward the end of the nineteenth century, many Jewish people emigrated to Palestine. By the end of the nineteenth century the population of Jewish people in the Palestinian area had doubled to around fifty thousand.[19]

During this same time a political movement known as Zionism began to take root. In 1896 a pamphlet entitled *The Jewish State (Der Judenstaat)* was published. Written by Theodor Herzl, *The Jewish State* described the creation of a modern, independent Jewish state. The following quote from the pamphlet I believe says it all:

> I believe that a wondrous generation of Jews will spring into existence. The Maccabeans will rise again. Let me repeat once more my opening words: The Jews who wish for a State will have it. We shall live at last as free men on our own soil, and die peacefully in our own homes. The world will be freed by our liberty, enriched by our wealth, magnified by our greatness. And whatever we attempt there to accomplish for our own welfare, will react powerfully and beneficially for the good of humanity.[20]

It was this sentiment that inspired many Jewish people to return to their homeland. Thus the movement of Zionism began. Zionism is basically a political movement originally aimed at the establishment of an independent Jewish state in Palestine and later aimed at the support of the nation of Israel as it exists today. Zionism grew to such proportions after the publication of *The Jewish State* that the first Zionist Congress was held in Basel, Switzerland, in 1897. Major aspects of Zionism are reflected in the Israeli Declaration of Independence. Here is an example:

> [The Land of Israel, Palestine] was the birthplace of the Jewish people. Here their spiritual, religious and political identity was shaped. Here they first attained to statehood, created cultural values of national and universal significance and gave to the world the eternal Book of Books.
>
> After being forcibly exiled from their land, the people kept faith with it throughout their Dispersion and never ceased to pray and hope for their return to it and for the restoration in it of their political freedom.
>
> Impelled by this historic and traditional attachment, Jews strove in every successive generation to re-establish themselves in their ancient homeland. In recent decades they returned in their masses.[21]

Another wave of Jewish immigration, known as the Second Aliyah, occurred between 1904 and 1914.[22] It occurred in the wake of a wave of pogroms in czarist Russia that were incited by the Russian government.[23] Jewish organizations from all over the world, such as the Jewish National Fund, collected donations so the emigrating Jews could buy land and create their own towns and cities to live in.[24] In 1909 the first kibbutz (a Jewish settlement or commune) was established.[25] Tel Aviv was founded the same year, and by the start of World War I in 1914 the Jewish population in Palestine had grown to around eighty-five thousand.[26]

JEWISH NATIONAL HOME

In 1917 the British army, under the leadership of General Edmund Allenby, succeeded in their operations against the Ottoman Empire and captured the city of Jerusalem. On November 2, 1917, British Foreign Secretary Arthur James Balfour issued what is known as the Balfour Declaration, indicating the British government's favorable view of "the establishment in Palestine of a national home for the Jewish people."[27]

Once World War I was over, the victorious Allies divided the spoils among themselves. League of Nations mandates granted France authorization to govern Syria and Lebanon, while mandates for Iraq and Palestine (including modern-day Israel and Jordan) were granted to Great Britain.[28] The mandate for Palestine included a provision for the establishment of a national home for the Jews in Palestine.[29]

Even though the Jewish people now had a national home, over the next thirty years they would face great resistance from their neighbors. April 1936 marked the start of a time period known as the Arab Revolt. The time period was marked by violence as Palestinian Arabs demanded the end of Jewish immigration to Palestine, the end of land sales to Jews, and the establishment of an Arab national government.[30] The revolt led to the White

Paper of 1939, a British government policy paper that limited Jewish immigration to Palestine and regulated the sale of Arab land to Jews.[31]

Tensions between the Jews and Arabs continued throughout World War II as many Jews illegally entered Palestine because of the Holocaust in Europe. When World War II ended in 1945, the United States gave its support to the Zionist cause. The British government, still operating under the mandate of Palestine, was not able to find a workable solution for Palestine and brought the problem to the United Nations. In November 1947 the United Nations voted to partition Palestine. On May 14, 1948, British forces withdrew from Palestine when the mandate expired; the Jews had already gained full control of the portion of Palestine granted to them by the United Nations.[32]

ISRAEL BECOMES A STATE

On May 14, 1948, David Ben-Gurion, the first prime minister of Israel, had the distinct pleasure of reading Israel's Declaration of Independence. Israel was now a sovereign nation! The next day the joint armies of Egypt, Syria, Lebanon, and Iraq invaded Israel.[33] The Arab forces lost the war, but Israel has been in a constant state of war with its neighbors ever since.

In all that Israel had to endure for more than 1,800 years, it took a miracle for them to survive as a people. Nevertheless, the promise and prophecy of Jesus Christ made it clear that Israel would return. The metaphorical budding of the fig tree happened as prophecy foretold. Israel's reemergence as a nation is our first marker on the prophetic timeline as we ask the question, how close are we?

Let's say that the end of the prophetic timeline is when we are raptured. We now know that our starting point is May 14, 1948, the date of Israel's return as a sovereign nation. Since we obviously haven't been raptured yet, we need to move the timeline up to see when the last rapture could be. We will be able to narrow the timeline down as we move along, for as Sir Arthur Conan Doyle's Sherlock Holmes said, "The game is afoot." [34]

Chapter 5
SIGNS OF THE TIME

NOW THAT WE know that Israel becoming a nation on May 14, 1948, was our first marker on the prophetic timeline, what's the next marker? Can we narrow the timeline down and get a better look at how close we are to the next rapture? We most certainly can.

When Jesus told us that Israel would return as a nation, He also gave us our next clue as to when the final rapture would happen and how close we really are. In each of the three gospels that recount the parable of the fig tree, Jesus said that "this generation will not pass away until all these things are fulfilled" (Luke 21:32; see also Matthew 24:34; Mark 13:30). The generation those passages are referring to is the generation that existed when Israel again became a nation. That generation Christ was referring to is alive in the time period you and I are presently living in. And I shall now prove it!

How Long Is a Generation?

To determine if we are living in the time period of the generation that saw the return of Israel as a sovereign nation, we need to figure out how long a biblical generation is. Depending upon which passages you're reading, a biblical generation can be 40, 60, 70, 80, or even 120 years long. The pre-Flood life span was around 900 years, and the average life span of those who lived shortly after the Flood dropped drastically to around 480 years.

So how do we determine which time span for a generation we should use? Let's apply a little bit of common sense and math to answer the question. To begin with, we shall automatically dismiss 480 years and 900 years from our list of possibilities. The reason is that those generations lived during a period of time in which life was normally much longer than it is today. In addition, the prophecy Christ gave us was a few thousand years after the time period of the Flood. When Christ walked the earth, a generation was much shorter, and it is those biblical generations we will look toward for an answer.

If we use the biblical measure for a generation of forty years, then the rapture should have occurred by 1988 because that would be one generation, or forty years, after Israel became a nation. Well, obviously that can't be the correct answer because the rapture did not happen by then. If we look at the next measurement of a biblical generation, sixty years, then the rapture should have occurred by 2008, sixty years after Israel became a nation. The rapture did not occur by then, so that can't be the answer.

What about using the biblical measurement of seventy or eighty years found in Psalm 90:10? Now that could work, because adding seventy to eighty years to 1948 would come out to be 2018 to 2028. If we add the highest number of years for a biblical generation based on current life spans, 120 years, then we end up with the year 2068.

Before going on any further, let me reiterate a scripture: "But concerning that day or hour no one knows, not even the angels in heaven, nor the Son, but only the Father"

(Mark 13:32). In that verse Jesus Christ pointed out that no knows when the next rapture will occur. No one knows the day or the hour—no man knows, the angels do not know, and even Christ Himself doesn't know. Only God the Father knows the exact moment He is going to turn to His Son and say, "Gather up My children."

THE DANGERS OF DATE SETTING

Scripture warns us that "God is not mocked" (Gal. 6:7). And considering the topic we are covering now—when the next and final rapture will occur—in light of God the Father stating that only He knows when the final rapture will occur, do not take it upon yourself to set a specific date for when it will happen. You are not God, you do not know the mind of God, and if you dare to mock God by date setting, you will indeed reap what you have sown.

There have been quite a number of date setters in the past who quite obviously were wrong in their predictions of when the next rapture will occur. A book could be written on that topic alone. Instead of doing that to prove our point, let's take a look at one fairly recent date setter.

Before saying anything else, please allow me to say this: I do not like to speak ill of the dead. It takes me out of my comfort zone, because only God has the right to judge anyone. However, for the sake of being a good and faithful Christian teacher, I must relate to you the following events.

Harold Camping was a Christian radio broadcaster, author, and evangelist. He predicted that Christ would return in September 1994.[1] It was a most dangerous thing to do because Camping usurped God, His Word, and His position as God when he (Camping) set a date for when

Christ would return. Once his prediction failed, Harold was thrust into the category of false prophet.

Deuteronomy 18:22 reads as follows: "When a prophet speaks in the name of the LORD, if the thing does not occur or come to pass, that is the thing which the LORD has not spoken; the prophet has spoken it presumptuously. You shall not be afraid of him." During the days of the Old Testament, a false prophet was usually stoned to death.

Yet Camping's false prophecies didn't end in 1994. For months leading up to May 21, 2011, Family Radio, of which Harold Camping was president, ran a publicity campaign stating Jesus Christ would return to Earth and we would be raptured. There would also be five months of earthquakes and fires following May 21, 2011.[2]

When the rapture did not occur on May 21, 2011, Camping stated that a "spiritual" judgment occurred on that date instead and the actual physical rapture would not occur until October 21, 2011, five months later.[3] Like so many other Christians I waited and watched for those five months, knowing that the rapture would not occur on that date. Once October 21, 2011 came and went, it was painfully obvious that Camping was wrong again.

It was the third time that Camping's predictions about the rapture and such were wrong. As a result of this third disaster, Camping was labeled a false prophet and Family Radio suffered a major loss of assets, staff, and revenue. Two years later, Harold Camping died.[4] But the year before he died, Harold repented of his sin and stated that his attempt to predict the rapture was sinful.[5]

If there is nothing else to learn from Harold Camping's predictions, we can learn that it is sinful and wrong to predict when the rapture will occur. When God told us that no one can know the day nor hour, He meant it!

Now without using any date-setting methods, let's go back to our timeline. Keeping in mind the divine warning that no one can know the day nor hour, can we at least try to guess at the season, the time in human history, when we know we're close? I believe that is possible, but we must be very careful how we do this. Date setting is against everything I stand for, and I know that God doesn't want date setting to be done either. So we will examine the signs we were told to look for, and from there we will try to figure out where we may be on the prophetic timeline. We will also take a look at past raptures to see if they can help us determine just how close we are to the next and final one.

Chapter 6
SIGNS IN THE PROPHETIC TIMELINE

THERE'S AN OLD axiom that states, "In order to understand the present, you must look to the past." And this is what we will do. We are going to look to the past and see if any of the ancient signs of a coming rapture are unfolding now.

We are going to be very specific in our examination and make a lot of comparisons in order to determine if we are witnessing genuine, biblical signs that herald the arrival of Christ in the clouds for the next rapture, or if we're looking at something that just happens in nature and can be easily explained away. I honestly believe the end results will shock a number of you and make you sit up, take notice, and seriously begin to ponder the times we're living in.

In chapter 3, "Biblical Examples of Raptures," we discovered that there were quite a number of raptures in the past:

- Noah and the Ark

- Lot and the Cities of Sodom and Gomorrah

- Moses and the Ten Plagues of Egypt

- Enoch's Removal

- Elijah and the Chariot of Fire

In order to determine if the prophetic past is catching up to the prophetic present and future, we're going to take a look at some of the events surrounding the ten plagues of Egypt when God, through Moses, confronted Pharaoh and his magicians, and determine if anything is truly going on in the prophetic realm.

Whenever Moses confronted Pharaoh, he had specific instructions from the Lord. When Pharaoh first asked Moses to do a miracle, Moses told Aaron to throw his rod on the ground. Aaron cast his rod down to the ground, and it became a serpent (Exod. 7:8–10). This was not one of the ten plagues of Egypt. This can best be understood as a warm-up; God was only just beginning to flex and show Pharaoh who really was in charge.

THE FIRST PLAGUE—
WATER TURNING INTO BLOOD

When Moses and Aaron followed the Lord's instructions and Aaron struck the waters with his rod, the waters of Egypt, including the Nile River, turned into blood for a full week. Is anything like that going on nowadays? Actually, yes, and in quite a number of geographical locations.

On November 27, 2012, it was reported that the water at Bondi Beach in Sydney, Australia, looked like blood.[1] Sydney's beaches were closed once again when the water turned blood red in early 2016.[2] On February 16, 2012, it was reported that the Beirut River in Lebanon had turned blood red, alarming local inhabitants and government officials.[3] Water also turned the color of blood in Brazil in 2015 and in Camargue, France, in 2012.[4]

The Yangtze River in China appeared blood red in 2012.

On July 24, 2014, a river in Cangnan county of Wenzhou, Zhejiang province, the water became the color of blood.[5] In late 2013 the river in Myjava, Slovakia, on the border to Czechia, turned into the bright red color of blood.[6] Similar events occurred along the Florida coast of the Gulf of Mexico in December 2015 and in other countries around the world.[7]

Remember, as pointed out earlier, the events surrounding the confrontation between Moses and Pharaoh constituted a rapture. So I am not surprised that there are similarities between a past rapture and what's going on today. What's even more interesting is that in the future, during the Tribulation, water will be turning into blood again—Revelation 8:8 and 16:3 make this abundantly clear.

THE SECOND PLAGUE—FROGS

The second plague of Egypt was frogs. It begs the question: Has anyone seen a plague of frogs lately? Actually, yes!

In June 2015 Ganjingzi Qu in China's Liaoning Province was overrun with thousands of toads after a heavy rainfall. There were so many toads that it looked as if the ground were moving.[8]

Videos from 2010 show Anderson Lake with what appears to be tens of thousands of frogs.[9] Another video from 2010 shows thousands of tiny frogs at Laguna Hanson in Baja California.[10]

THE THIRD AND FOURTH PLAGUES— LICE AND FLIES

Have there been any plagues of lice or flies lately?

In Exodus 8:16 we find that Aaron stretched out his rod

and struck the ground. Immediately the dust turned into lice and did so throughout all of Egypt. Let's look at the third plague of lice and compare it to today's events and see if anything similar is happening now.

In August 2016 a lice study reported that forty-two out of forty-eight states tested were overrun by what was being termed "super lice"—lice that is resistant to over-the-counter treatments.[11] This was a significant increase from the twenty-five states reporting super lice in February 2016.[12] Normal lice treatments, known as pyrethroids, were 100 percent effective back in 2000.[13] But in August 2016, 100 percent of the lice tested in those forty-two states were resistant to over-the-counter treatments. It seems that ordinary lice mutated and built up a resistance to conventional treatments.[14] Egypt was afflicted with a plague of lice; this is a biblical and historical fact. However, Egypt's plague was nothing in comparison to the geographical area afflicted by lice in the United States.

Beyond any shadow of a doubt the outbreak of super lice is a reality. But what about the fifth plague of Egypt—flies? Lice is common enough, but there has also recently been an outbreak of a disease carried by mosquitos. A mosquito-borne illness known as the Zika virus has spread throughout more than eighty countries in Africa, Asia, North America (especially Central America and the Caribbean), and South America. The World Health Organization declared the Zika virus a public health emergency in 2016. The Zika virus is similar to other mosquito-borne viruses such as yellow fever, West Nile fever, and so forth. The virus may also affect babies in their mothers' wombs, and there are studies going on right now to determine the overall effects of the Zika virus.[15]

Is there anything else that has gone on in recent years that we could compare to the biblical plague of flies? In 2014 an event referred to as a "bugnado" was photographed in Portugal. Large swarms of insects in the shape of a swirling vortex are being spotted in locations around the world. They are similar in appearance to a tornado but are made up of insects, such as red locusts or midges.[16] While perhaps not quite on the scale of the plague of flies that afflicted Egypt, the "bugnadoes" certainly are at least reminiscent of the plague.

THE FIFTH PLAGUE—
LIVESTOCK DISEASE

The fifth plague of Egypt, diseased animals (possibly anthrax), is found in Exodus 9:1–7. Interestingly enough, only in the last twenty-five to thirty years have we seen anthrax with such devastating results.

Anthrax is a very ugly, destructive disease that has devastating and painful results on those poor animals stricken with such a disease. During the 2016 anthrax outbreak in western Siberia, ninety people were hospitalized and a twelve-year-old child died. The sudden outbreak also hit the local reindeer population and killed over two thousand of them.[17] Another similar disease to consider is foot-and-mouth disease. In early 2001 an outbreak of foot-and-mouth disease in the United Kingdom led to the slaughter of almost four million animals, leading to the loss of hundreds of millions of dollars and decimating the agricultural industry.[18] Suffice it to say that anthrax, foot-and-mouth disease, and other such diseases are found both in the distant past and today. They are destructive to both livestock and humans.

THE SIXTH PLAGUE—BOILS

I doubt that there is any real biblical connection, but because of the present war going on with Islamic Jihadists throughout the world, chemical warfare is being used. Often chemical weapons produce boils on the bodies of victims. During World War I alone over ninety thousand deaths were attributed to poison gas.[19] Though more recent chemical warfare attacks, such as the 1995 sarin attack in Tokyo, were not biblical in their execution, I still find it no small coincidence that boils might be on the list of the things beginning to happen during this time period we're living in. It is also quite possible that the grievous sores referred to in Revelation 16 are the result of chemical warfare (vv. 2, 10–11).

THE SEVENTH PLAGUE—HAIL

In Exodus 9:13–35 we find that Moses stretched out his hands to the sky and brought forth hail. But it was no ordinary hail—it was mingled with fire. How can fire and ice coexist? Normally they don't, but this was an act of the divine will of God.

Hail is normally as small as or smaller than a marble. However, larger hailstones can cause serious damage or even death.

On August 10, 2011, hail that was three inches in diameter was reported in Sterling, Colorado.[20] For comparison, take a look at a baseball and you'll really begin to understand how serious the hailstorm was. Keep in mind that a hailstone the size of a baseball is estimated to fall as fast as one hundred miles per hour.[21]

The largest hailstone on record in the United States weighed almost two pounds and had a diameter of eight inches.[22] Can you imagine hail that size landing on someone's home? It would smash its way through the roof of the home with ease. And heaven help anyone who was outside when such a storm hit.

In the future God will once again use hail to punish the sinful and disobedient inhabitants of Earth. Revelation 16:21 (KJV) says there will be a plague of hail with hailstones weighing about a talent each. A biblical talent weighed about seventy-five pounds. That is equivalent to five bowling balls. Imagine hail of that size falling down at over one hundred miles per hour and crashing into the ground below. Think of how deep such hailstones would imbed themselves in the earth. Now imagine millions of hailstones dropping down on everything on the planet as a part of God's divine judgment. What a horrific scene those poor folks living during the Tribulation will face.

I am not saying that this is precisely what happened in Egypt when Moses called down the hail, but as it was a judgment of God and was referred to as a plague, it is at least a possibility that the hailstones were massive. And let's not forget that each of the hailstones was also on fire. Read Exodus 9:13–35 and Revelation 16:21 for yourself and see what seems to be a definitive connection between the past and the future, and consider the signs we see in the present.

THE EIGHTH PLAGUE—LOCUSTS

Among the most destructive forces on the face of the earth are locust swarms. By itself a locust is a harmless grasshopper that happily eats any sort of plant life. But when locusts swarm, no vegetation is left behind. Your best recourse in the middle of such a swarm is to stay inside and pray that something green is left behind. But the odds are there will be nothing left, just as occurred when locusts covered the land of Egypt (Exod. 10:13–15).

Just as with other plagues of Egypt, we see signs of locust plagues in recent history. A March 2013 article reported that "at least twenty swarms of locusts, each comprising up to 80 million insects, have invaded Egypt over the past three months." Needless to say, crops were decimated, as a single swarm of locusts can consume as many as one hundred thousand tons of crops.[23]

In 2013 Madagascar suffered its worst swarms of locusts since the 1950s, with locusts infesting more than half of the country's cultivated land.[24] A state of emergency was declared in southern Russia in 2015 when millions of locusts destroyed at least 10 percent of the farmland in the area.[25] In early 2016 Argentina faced the "worst plague of locusts in more than half a century." The locusts spread across an area the size of Delaware.[26]

Other devastating swarms of locusts have been reported in other countries in recent years as well. This may also be a sign of the times.

THE NINTH PLAGUE—DARKNESS

The Bible teaches us that God caused a great darkness to fall upon Egypt for three days (Exod. 10:21–29). The darkness was so great, it could be felt (Exod. 10:21). This particular God-ordained event was not a solar nor a lunar eclipse. Here's why: The length of this event was three days. This in and of itself means that it was not a solar or a lunar eclipse, because solar eclipses last seven and a half minutes or less (once the sun is completely covered) and lunar eclipses last around two hours (once the moon is completely covered).[27]

The event must have been a local event because there are no other records around the world that spoke of such a three-day event in any other geographical location. And it's not as if such an event would have gone unnoticed in any other country had the darkness been anything other than a local event.

Over the last few years there has been a major brouhaha over what has been called the "Four Blood Moons," properly called the "Lunar Eclipse Tetrad," when you have four total lunar eclipses in a row. Many—and I do mean many—announcements were made and events were held during 2014 and 2015 regarding this astrological event, which lasted for almost a year and a half. Some said the four blood moons heralded the final rapture. Others actually predicted doomsday would arrive. Still others declared that the blood moons held some sort of prophetic meaning because they landed on Jewish feast days as most blood moons in the past were not connected to Jewish feast days.

On many radio shows throughout 2014 and 2015 I stated that I thought it was all rubbish. And I still do. The main reason I believe it was nothing but rubbish was because I looked at other lunar eclipse tetrads in the past. I went back more than one thousand years, and not all of the blood moons happened on Jewish feast days.

It was also said that every time a blood moon occurred, something major that could be of historical significance happened to the Jews. I applied a little common sense as I traced the blood moon events backwards in time, and history showed me that an event that could be construed as monumental or historical only happened a few times. In fact, many people stated that a blood moon occurred when this Jewish war happened or when that monumental Jewish event happened, and so on and so forth. Again, that is not accurate. The truth of the matter is that sometimes a blood moon occurred around the time of a Jewish war or some other monumental event affecting the Jews. However, the blood moon happened either before the event or after it, not exactly on the day of the event. For this reason alone you simply cannot put any real divine significance to the blood moons. This is not a game of horseshoes where you can get points for being close to the peg. No! If this was of God, it would be dead on, a ringer. God does not operate by being close enough or in the neighborhood of being right. God is perfect, and the blood moons were anything but perfect as far as always landing on a feast day or some historical event involving the Jewish people. So again, for the record, the blood moons were not a direct sign from God.

Even though the blood moons were not a direct sign from God, I can honestly state that they could be a warning sign from God of things to come. The reason I believe this could be true is that we know that darkness struck Egypt for three days.

During the Tribulation God will strike the throne of the beast and his kingdom with darkness (Rev. 16:10). Note very carefully that the Bible does not say that the whole earth will be stricken with darkness. It says only the throne of the beast and his kingdom—in other words the headquarters out of which he operates. That would make this future plague of darkness another localized event as it was in the past with Pharaoh and Egypt.

Revelation 16:10 is also very reminiscent of what happened in Egypt because the darkness is going to be so intense that people will literally bite down on their tongues. I know when I've accidentally bitten my tongue, it was quite painful. Now imagine those poor folks during the Tribulation who are going to purposely gnaw on and bite their tongues. This is how great and how intense the darkness is going to be for them.

Ecclesiastes 1:9 reads, "What has been is the same as what will be, and what has been done is the same as what will be done; there is nothing new under the sun." This verse tells us many different things. "What has been is the same as what will be" means what is happening now has already happened in the past. "What has been done is the same as what will be done" means what is happening now shall happen again in the future. "There is nothing new under the sun" is very, very true because history repeats itself over and over again as we fail to learn the lessons of the past. And until we do learn from the past, nothing is ever really going to change. We will constantly make the same mistakes over and over again.

We have only just begun our prophetic journey. In trying to understand how close we are to the next rapture, we looked into the past to determine if there were any events that were similar to events happening now in our lifetime. In particular we examined the ancient events that occurred when Moses confronted Pharaoh, and we were able to figure a couple of things out. A number of the plagues were very similar to events that have happened during recent years. This is very important to note because a rapture occurred during the confrontation between Moses and Pharaoh. Since we see a number of similar events beginning to occur, we should be moving even closer to when the next rapture will occur.

We also learned that a number of the events that occurred during the plagues of Egypt will also occur outside of our lifetime during the Tribulation. Therefore, we do know that history will repeat and God will use many of the same plagues He used to garner the attention of the Egyptians to get the attention of those living during the Tribulation.

Again, we have only just begun our prophetic journey. We will now examine many prophecies to determine just how close we really are to the final rapture. And as I like to do at home, break out the popcorn and a drink because we have only just begun to scratch the surface of prophecy.

Chapter 7
WARS AND RUMORS OF WARS

THE RETURN OF Israel as a nation was the first sign on the prophetic timeline. Scripture teaches us that the Jewish people that were held captive in the past were gathered and returned to Israel. Isaiah 11:11–12 reads, "In that day the LORD shall set His hand again the second time to recover the remnant of His people.... He shall set up a banner for the nations, and shall assemble the outcasts of Israel, and gather together the dispersed of Judah from the four corners of the earth." The Jewish people, as prophesied, were gathered and returned to Israel after the Babylonian captivity. (The implied first time, they were recovered by the hand of the Lord.)

However, the Jewish people rejected the Messiah, Jesus Christ, and they were once again dispersed. This time their dispersion was because they rejected the Messiah. Jesus foretold, "They will fall by the edge of the sword and will be led away captive to all nations. And Jerusalem will be trampled on by the Gentiles until the times of the Gentiles are fulfilled" (Luke 21:24). We know this prophecy was fulfilled when Titus besieged Jerusalem in AD 70 and the Jewish people were once again scattered to different parts of the world.

ISRAEL AS
A MODERN NATION

Once the Jewish folks went through a diaspora of almost nineteen centuries, they returned once again to Israel as prophesied. Isaiah 66:7–8 reads, "Before she was in labor, she gave birth; before her pain came, she delivered a son. Who has heard such a thing? Who has seen such things? Shall the earth be made to give birth in one day? Shall a nation be born at once? For as soon as Zion was in labor, she brought forth her sons." Israel was born as a modern nation in one day when it became a sovereign state on May 14, 1948. The prophecy was fulfilled!

We find another prophecy about God's deliverance of His chosen nation in Zechariah 8:4–8:

> Thus says the LORD of Hosts: Older men and women will again sit in the streets of Jerusalem, each having a staff in his hand because of advanced age. And the plazas of the city will be filled with young boys and girls playing in her open places. Thus says the LORD of Hosts: If it is marvelous in the eyes of the remnant of this people in these days, will it also be marvelous in My eyes? says the LORD of Hosts. Thus says the LORD of Hosts: I will deliver My people from the eastern lands and from the western lands. And I will bring them, and they will reside in Jerusalem, and they will be for Me as a people, and I will be for them as God, with faithfulness and righteousness.

During the Six-Day War, which began on June 5, 1967, God again delivered His chosen nation as prophesied so long ago. There are many stories of miracles that happened during the Six-Day War. I suggest that you look them up on the Internet if you're interested and see what you may discover.

Another prophecy that helps us determine where we are on the prophetic timeline and how close we are to the rapture stated that there would be great political unrest aimed directly toward Israel: "I am going to make Jerusalem a cup of reeling before all the surrounding nations. And when there is a siege against Judah, it is also against Jerusalem. And it will be on that day that I will set Jerusalem as a weighty stone to all the peoples. All who carry it will surely gash themselves, and all the nations of the land will be gathered against it" (Zech. 12:2–3). Right now, beyond any shadow of a doubt, it appears as if the nations of the earth are slowly gathering and uniting against Israel. Even our own government, which has long been pro-Israel, under the Obama administration allowed the United Nations to condemn Israel and released hundreds of millions of dollars to the Palestinian Authority.[1] I can only pray Donald Trump's administration will do better.

WARS AND
THE FULFILLMENT OF PROPHECY

The Gospel of Matthew tells us that Jesus said, "You will hear of wars and rumors of wars. See that you are not troubled. For all these things must happen, but the end is not yet. For nation will rise against nation, and kingdom against kingdom. There will be famines, epidemics, and earthquakes in various places. All these are the beginning of sorrows" (Matt. 24:6–8).

Next we turn to the Gospel of Mark. Jesus said, "When

you hear of wars and rumors of wars, do not be troubled. For such things must happen, but the end is still to come. For nation will rise against nation, and kingdom against kingdom. And there will be earthquakes in various places, and there will be famines and troubles. These are the beginning of sorrows" (Mark 13:7–8).

Now let's take a look at the Gospel of Luke. It tells us that Jesus said, "When you hear of wars and commotions, do not be afraid. For these things must first take place, but the end will not be at hand...Nation will rise against nation, and kingdom against kingdom. Great earthquakes will occur in various places, and there will be famines and pestilence. And there will be terrors and great signs from heaven" (Luke 21:9–11).

We have the same testimony from three different writers in the Bible, and from the Scriptures we know that it takes the testimony of two or three witnesses to establish facts. What I'm going to do now is revisit those warnings because they play a critical part in prophecy and in the events we have been witnessing for ourselves in recent years.

When we consider "wars and rumors of wars," I am convinced that no one could deny that prophetic warning is being fulfilled in our day and age. Ever since 9/11, when the Twin Towers of the World Trade Center were brought down by radical terrorists from the Middle East, the United States has been in an undeclared state of war. Terrorism continues to be an ongoing threat.

On November 12, 2014, Russian tanks, armored personnel carriers, and heavy artillery accompanied by Russian soldiers crossed the border into Ukraine. Similar incursions had been occurring since February.[2] Tensions between Ukraine and Russia have continued despite diplomatic intervention, and the situation has been referred to as the Ukraine Crisis.[3]

Iran continues to pose a threat to the United States and other countries despite President Obama's nuclear deal. When President Trump condemned Iran's January 2017 ballistic missile test, General Mohammad Pakpour, the commander of Iran's Revolutionary Guard, stated, "The enemy [the United States] should not be mistaken in its assessments and it will receive a strong slap in the face if it does make such a mistake."[4]

North Korea is presently being led by a madman known as Kim Jong-Un. In September 2016 North Korea claimed success with its fifth nuclear bomb test. Despite multiple UN sanctions since its first nuclear test in 2006, North Korea has continued to develop its nuclear program and test nuclear devices.[5] Kim Jong-Un has threatened to attack the United States and other countries on numerous occasions. He even had propaganda videos created that show missile attacks on targets in the United States.[6]

We can add to those the war in Afghanistan, the Iraqi civil war, the Mexican drug war, the Syrian civil war, the Kurdish-Turkish conflict, the Somali civil war, and many others. There is no doubt that the current time period fulfills the prophecy of wars and rumors of wars.

GOD'S CREATION REBELS: EARTHQUAKES

The Gospels of Matthew, Mark, and Luke warned us about earthquakes, famines, epidemics, and other catastrophic occurrences. These occurrences are God's creation rebelling. When I speak of God's creation in rebellion, I am referring to events that appear on the surface as natural or unnatural events. For example, as Christ was dying upon the cross, certain events happened that were not natural to the normal way of thinking. There was an eclipse that lasted three hours, the veil in the Temple was torn straight down the middle without any physical explanation, there was an earthquake, rocks split in two, and graves broke open and the bodies of departed saints rose (Matt. 27:51–52; Luke 23:44–45). Creation was in a state of rebellion against what we consider to be normal. In this instance, from my personal perspective, creation was rebelling because it could not accept the fact that the One who called it into existence was now dying. It is examples such as these that I am referring to when I speak of God's creation rebelling.

So the Gospels tell us that there will be earthquakes, but they will not be just ordinary earthquakes. The Gospel of Luke tells us that they would be "great" earthquakes. From what I understand, any earthquake with a magnitude of 6.0 or above is considered to be a major event. We will examine a number of earthquakes so that you can begin to see that the Scriptures are spot on—earthquakes are occurring around the world.

The Solomon Islands are located to the east of Papua New Guinea and consist of six major islands and over nine hundred smaller ones. But disaster hit this tropical paradise. On January 3, 2010, the islands were hit with a 7.1 magnitude earthquake.[7] The devastation that struck that lush region was almost unimaginable.

A few years later history repeated itself. On February 6, 2013, a magnitude 8.0 earthquake struck off the coast of the Solomon Islands. The earthquake was powerful enough to send a tsunami straight toward the island. The end results were as expected—many homes were destroyed, and several thousand people were affected.[8]

The nation of Chile runs just about the entire length of the western side of South America on the Pacific Ocean. On February 27, 2010, a magnitude 8.8 earthquake struck Chile. The force of the earthquake was so horrific that many buildings looked as if two gigantic hands raised themselves up out of the ground and ripped those buildings in two. The powerful earthquake was so strong that it created a tsunami that reached the coasts of Japan, New Zealand, California, and Hawaii.[9]

Sumatra is one of the five major islands of Indonesia in the Indian Ocean. On April 6, 2010, a magnitude 7.8 earthquake hit the island. On May 9, 2010, a 7.2 magnitude earthquake struck Sumatra. On March 2, 2016, a magnitude 7.8 earthquake occurred just to the southwest of the island.[10]

While earthquakes are a clear sign of the fulfillment of prophecy, they simply are not enough to make the point that God's creation appears to be in severe rebellion. Other things need to be happening around the same time frame before we can truly say this is part of the prophecies that God gave to us through the Bible. Therefore, let's take a look at some of the other forces that are being released upon mankind and the planet Earth.

GOD'S CREATION REBELS: VOLCANOES

One of the most destructive forces upon the face of the earth is the volcano. Volcanoes are easily capable of releasing more than one hundred times the destructive force of the atom bombs that were dropped upon Hiroshima and Nagasaki during World War II. Whole islands have been destroyed by volcanic eruptions.

Iceland is an island country that rests in between the north Atlantic Ocean and the Arctic Ocean. It is considered to be the most sparsely populated country in Europe. While part of Iceland is positively breathtaking, other parts are equally uninviting. In March 2010, the Eyjafjallajokull volcano in Iceland began erupting. On April 14, 2010, it began to explosively erupt. It was both a spectacular sight and a most frightful one. The eruption threw so much smoke and ash into the air that it brought European air travel to a standstill for over a week.[11] I remember that a friend of mine who was in the military at the time told me that even military flights were canceled because the soot and ash could clog up the engines of their airplanes.

As mesmerizing as volcanoes can be, they are nothing to take lightly or fool around with. They have wiped whole cities and towns off the face of the earth.

During the days of the apostles there was an ancient Roman city known as Pompeii. In its heyday Pompeii was a thriving vacation spot for Roman citizens. On August 24, 79, Mount Vesuvius erupted and completely destroyed Pompeii, Herculaneum, and a number of other places in the surrounding region. The destruction was so complete that Pompeii was buried underneath fourteen to seventeen feet of volcanic ash and pumice. The excavation of Pompeii told of a night of abject horror as people were buried alive. Many hung on to family members as they were either roasted alive by a pyroclastic cloud or suffocated to death.

All told, when Mount Vesuvius released its destructive forces on Pompeii, thousands of people died.[12]

Some might argue that those eruptions were in the past. Are there any volcanoes erupting nowadays? Sadly, yes. Several dozen volcanoes are erupting around the world.[13]

Why have I mentioned volcanoes, since they are not part of the signs of which Matthew, Mark, and Luke spoke? It is a scientific fact that many volcanoes are preceded by earthquakes. I personally believe the prophesied earthquakes will likely be followed by volcanic eruptions.

Revelation 6:12 teaches us that there is going to be a great earthquake. In verse 14 it tells us that the heavens are going to roll back as a scroll would, and that every mountain and island will be moved out of its normal place. If I wanted to ascribe these events to something that is normally found in nature, I would say that the great earthquake spoken of in Revelation 6:12 could produce such events.

GOD'S CREATION REBELS: EPIDEMICS AND FAMINE

Another sign of nature rebelling against mankind is epidemics or pestilences, what we would call plagues or diseases. When it comes to plagues, we have already made a comparison between the ten plagues of Egypt and events that are going on today. But what about diseases? We were also warned in Matthew 24 and Luke 21 of epidemics or pestilence.

Considering my medical background, I really don't feel it's necessary to get into diseases. There are so many diseases that have struck the earth, I wouldn't even know where to begin with it all. Suffice it to say that the signs of pestilences and epidemics are abundant. So that prophetic sign is definitely being seen.

I am also going to add famines to the list of prophetic signs that are being seen. Famine continues to be an issue. As of February 2017 twenty million people worldwide were categorized as on the brink of famine. Many of those twenty million are children facing imminent death.[14] What is truly sad is that America, the one nation that could help feed the whole world, has people who are starving to death also. Where are the children of the Most High God who are supposed to be feeding the hungry, visiting those in prison, helping the widows, and so on? I have been hungry a number of times in this life because I had no money to pay for food. By the grace of God, that is no longer the case. But I make it a practice in my home that whether you're friend, foe, relative, or stranger, I will always feed you if you show up on my doorstep and say you're hungry. No one should ever feel the pangs of hunger.

The passages we looked at in the Gospels also warned that famines would be among the signs to watch for before the return of the Lord. Because there is so much hunger worldwide right now, I really don't think I need to try and point out the signs of famine to anyone; they should be obvious to anyone.

Are there any other signs that we should be watching for other than diseases, famines, volcanoes, and earthquakes? Yes, and we will pick up this thought in the next chapter.

Chapter 8
COSMIC SIGNS

THE PASSAGE IN Luke that warned about earthquakes, famines, and pestilence also warned that there would be "terrors and great signs from heaven" (Luke 21:11). Before going on with this any further, allow me to give you a lesson from my days back at Louisiana Baptist University, when I was but a mere child in the Lord. In Christian high schools, colleges, and universities it is commonly taught that there are three heavens mentioned in the Bible:

- The first heaven is the immediate atmosphere surrounding the earth.

- The second heaven is outer space, the physical universe outside of Earth's atmosphere, including the sun, moon, stars, and planets.

- The third heaven is the actual abode of God Himself, wherever that may be.

Please don't get me started in a debate about the fourth and fifth dimensions, or we'll be here for the next month. Suffice it to say, those are the three heavens that are spoken of in the Bible.

The main reason I needed to give you a quick explanation about the three heavens is because when Luke 21:11

tells us there will be "terrors and great signs from heaven," the word *heaven* is referring to the immediate atmosphere surrounding the earth, the sky above us. I believe that the *terrors and great signs* mentioned in Luke 21:11 could very well be comets, meteors, or asteroids. And I do have sound reasoning for my belief.

From Revelation 8:8–9 we find out that "something like a great mountain, burning with fire" will be cast into the sea (the salt water of the earth), turning one-third of the water to blood, killing one-third of the sea creatures, and destroying one-third of the ships. Then in the next two verses, Revelation 8:10–11, we discover that a "great star from heaven, burning like a torch" will strike one-third of the rivers and springs (the fresh water of the earth) and turn them into a poison known as wormwood, which will cause the death of many people. The great mountain and the star could very well be comets, asteroids, or meteors.

Now considering the topic of discussion, the next logical question should be, Are there any comets, meteors, or asteroids falling out of the heavens nowadays that we could consider as partially or completely fulfilling the prophecies found in the Book of Luke? Not surprisingly, yes, there are. Asteroids, meteors, and comets are showing up in numbers that we have never seen before.

In July 1994 the comet Shoemaker-Levy 9 headed straight for the planet Jupiter. This particular comet was trapped by Jupiter's orbit and was on a one-way course of destruction. Shoemaker-Levy 9 had previously been torn into pieces when it neared Jupiter two years before.[1] Scientists around the world were having a field day because no one had ever seen a comet strike any of the planets in our solar system.[2] But the destruction that

Shoemaker-Levy 9 caused eventually garnered the attention of the United States Congress. From July 16, 1994, to July 22, 1994, twenty-one separate pieces of Shoemaker-Levy 9 collided with Jupiter. The damage left in its wake was on a scale never seen before.[3] Many photos of Jupiter were taken using the Hubble telescope and other powerful telescopes. Some of the photos were ultraviolet and gave us a much better look at how vast and destructive one comet can be.

Dark spots were left behind on Jupiter after the Shoemaker-Levy 9 comet fragments impacted the planet. One of those dark spots was around the size of Earth.[4] Yes! You did read that correctly. Had the fragment of the Shoemaker-Levy 9 comet that left behind such a dark spot on Jupiter struck us, you wouldn't be reading this book right now.

What I find sad and amusing is that there were some folks who told me there still wasn't anything to be concerned about because the Shoemaker-Levy 9 comet impacting Jupiter was a one-in-a-million chance event. I knew something prophetic was happening before our very eyes, but I was told it was nothing significant. Oh, really? In July 2009 Jupiter was struck again by an asteroid.[5] So much for a one-in-a-million chance.

On July 19, 2009, Anthony Wesley of Australia observed the black spot indicating that Jupiter had been struck by an asteroid. If you can, jaunt over to the Internet and take a look at the photos of the impact near Jupiter's south pole. The impact was the size of the Pacific Ocean.[6] Anthony Wesley was also the first one to observe yet another impact that occurred on June 3, 2010.[7] And if you can believe it, an amateur astronomer took some footage of Jupiter on

September 10, 2012, as it was being struck yet again by an asteroid or comet.[8]

An argument could be made that it was only Jupiter that was struck by four cosmic objects. Jupiter is the largest planet in our solar system and would naturally pull in such objects due to its phenomenal gravitational forces, and as such we don't have anything to worry about. But let's not forget the fact that Revelation 8 warns that there will be two such cosmic events. Revelation 8:8 says a "great mountain, burning with fire" will strike the sea. This is extremely critical to understand: one-third of all sea creatures shall die and one-third of all the ships will be destroyed. The question is, why? The answer is obvious. Any object as big as an asteroid, comet, or meteor that hits the oceans of the world will instantly create a tidal wave hundreds of feet, if not more than one thousand feet, in height. Think of the damage that such a tidal wave would cause around the world. The death toll could be phenomenal because as of 2010, people living in coastal areas represented 37 percent of the world's population.[9] If we combine that with a third of the fresh water being contaminated (Rev. 8:10–11), literally hundreds of millions could die as a result of the objects that will strike the waters as prophesied in the Book of Revelation.

Near Misses for Earth

In the last dozen years or so many asteroids barely missed hitting planet Earth by astronomical measurements. On November 6, 2009, an asteroid passed in between the moon and Earth. As I recall, it missed us by around 8,700 miles. What's really scary is that we didn't see that one coming.[10]

On February 15, 2013, asteroid 2013 DA14 missed impacting Earth by about 17,000 miles.[11] And on September 7, 2014, asteroid 2014 RC missed hitting Earth by only 24,800 miles.[12]

There have been dozens of other near misses over the last dozen years, but the one I want to turn your attention to next is Apophis. In December 2004 an asteroid known as 99942 Apophis caused a swell of concern in the scientific community. Early calculations indicated that there was a 2.7 percent chance that Apophis would strike Earth on April 13, 2029. Further observation came up with better measurements stating that Apophis would not impact either the Earth or the moon in 2029; however, there remained a slight possibility that Apophis would strike a very small region of Earth's atmosphere, bounce off, and return seven years later to impact the Earth directly in 2036. Fortunately in 2013 it was determined that Apophis has no chance of striking planet Earth. And we indeed are most fortunate. Apophis is approximately 690 to 1,080 feet in length.[13] Think of the global disasters it could cause if it were to strike our planet.

The fearful sights and great signs from heaven we were warned about could also happen in a number of other ways. Think of solar flares and coronal mass ejections. Any coronal mass ejection that is large enough could bring down the entire power grid of the earth.[14]

Gamma-ray bursts are also of concern. A gamma-ray burst is an electromagnetic explosion believed to be caused by a supernova. The gamma-ray burst emits more energy in a single burst than the sun has emitted in its entire lifetime.[15] That is something I can barely wrap my mind around. Still, if we were ever struck by one of those gamma-ray bursts, our entire way of life could be permanently changed.

We take so much for granted, never considering how dangerous the universe truly can be. It is only because of God's divine perfection in His creation that we haven't been destroyed by any cosmic calamities, and by the grace of God we as born-again Christians never will be. However, in the past God has used His creation to punish people on the earth, and in the near future He will turn His creation against the people on the earth again during the Tribulation. So we need to be about our Father's business and witness to as many as we can before time runs out and we are raptured. We need to save as many folks as we can before it is too late.

Chapter 9
FALSE SIGNS AND WONDERS

WHEN THE DISCIPLES asked Christ when He would be coming back, the Lord gave them a list of things to look for: famines, pestilence, troubles, terror, and great signs. (See Matthew 24; Mark 13; Luke 21.) We have already discussed possible natural disasters that the Lord warned us to look for, such as earthquakes and possibly even volcanoes. We were also warned to look for what I call cosmic calamities, such as asteroids, meteors, or comets—those things referred to in the Bible as terrors and great signs from heaven (Luke 21:11). Over the last few chapters we also discussed what could very well be divine reminders of some of the plagues and miracles that occurred in the past and appear to be happening yet again in this day and age, such as water appearing to turn to blood, hailstorms, and plagues of locusts.

Along the way we also discussed the fulfillment of prophecy—the total destruction of the Jewish Temple, the Jewish people being scattered to the four corners of the world, and what I believe is the most important prophecy: the return of Israel as a modern nation after the Jewish people have been scattered for hundreds of years. Prophecy will always have its way! That's a fact.

Now we need to begin to consider false signs and wonders. Certain things are happening around the world that many people consider to be acts of God. While many signs are definitely indicative of the clear fulfillment of biblical prophecy, others appear to have a supernatural origin not necessarily connected to any specific prophecy. Nevertheless, I feel that it's necessary to visit some of them because they could very well be indicators of God moving once again to gain the attention of His people and remind them what could very well happen shortly.

BEAMS OF LIGHT

Throughout the world mysterious beams of light have been seen. As Christians I believe we need to examine these phenomena because we are to be ever vigilant to the deceptions of the enemy. And as with anything else, once we have examined certain events, we should be able to determine if they are of the enemy or not. Beams of light are appearing around the world—that is a fact. And because they could have a supernatural element to them, we need to determine if these events are of God or of the enemy.

The ancient Mayan civilization ruled over what is now Mexico and Central America hundreds of years ago. They built some of the most incredible cities of the ancient world. The ancient cities had roadways that ran throughout them, huge astrological observatories with round domes such as you would expect to see in modern-day astronomical observatories, and step pyramids. It's the pyramids that are the most mysterious of all the ancient structures.

We know that the great pyramid found in Chichen Itza was used for the rites of human sacrifice.[1] But another mystery appeared involving Chichen Itza. A photo surfaced that showed a mysterious beam of light shooting straight up from the top of the pyramid and into the heavens. The

photo went viral because of the Mayan doomsday predictions.[2] Everyone was trying to figure out what that mysterious beam of light was. What was its purpose? Did the
pyramid contain some sort of power that had only recently
been activated? If so, what were the ancient Mayans trying
to tell us? Could they be telling us that we were about to
face some sort of doomsday scenario? After all, December
21, 2012, the date when the earth was supposed to face
some sort of doomsday scenario based on the Mayan cal-
endar, was fast approaching. It was for this reason that an
abnormally high amount of attention was paid to Chichen
Itza and the mysterious beam of light. Was the beam of
light some sort of cosmic sign from the heavens?

Yet even though the world was supposed to come to an
end in 2012, nothing happened. And in reality the photo
was just the result of a glitch on the photographer's phone.
The man who took the photo even acknowledged that
the beam of light was not visible when he was looking at
the pyramid; it only appeared in the photo.[3] It turns out
that the rolling shutter on cameras often produces a similar beam of light when lightning is being photographed.[4]
If you're interested, there are many good articles on the
Internet that thoroughly explain the rolling shutter effect.
The religious fervor and worry produced in 2012 over a
photographic glitch is another reason why we should
never try to date set.

There was another photo about which many people con-
tacted me. This particular photo was of a massive beam of
light streaming down from heaven onto the earth beneath.
People wanted to know if that beam of light was a sign
from God. I can assure you that the photo was once again
the result of the rolling shutter effect.

In my files I have photos in which a beam of light is breaking through some heavy cloud cover. This is actually the sun breaking through a tiny opening in the clouds and creating a beam of light. It appears as such because the clouds are not fully opened and only a concentrated sliver of light breaks through. With the right colors in the background, such events are truly spectacular to behold, but they are not some sort of sign from God. They are merely part of the creation of God; they are a natural event.

In the past there have been many beams of light that can quite easily be explained away. However, in Japan in 2012 a photo of a beam appeared that to this very day still has no explanation.[5] And quite honestly, I can't figure this one out. None of the usual explanations can tell us what it really was. It remains a mystery as far as I'm aware. But it was the widest beam of light I saw in any photo.

There are those who believe, and on parts of this I must concur, that some of the beams of light may be due to Project Blue Beam, which involves light refractions and holograms. Some believe Project Blue Beam will be used to create a false rapture, but that part I don't see happening, let alone fitting in with the plans of the Illuminati. Oh, they are going to create a cover story for the rapture, but the Illuminati's plans to cover up the rapture involves a false alien visitation, not holograms. Project Blue Beam will be used for something different, as you will soon find out.

While some beams of light do have natural explanations to them, others do not. And some of them are a direct result of Project Blue Beam.

LIGHT REFRACTION

False images can happen in another way—through light refraction. How many times have we driven down the highway and seen a mirage in front of us? A mirage is merely the result of intense heat on the ground refracting the light in such a way that it temporarily creates a mirrorlike effect. That is why we see either our car or someone else's reflected on the roadway. Other false images can be created by suspended raindrops in the atmosphere after a rainstorm.

What seemed to be a floating city appeared in China in June 2011 from the mist rising in the middle of the Xin'an River. The mist refracted the light and created an optical illusion of a so-called floating city.[6] Another seemingly floating city appeared in Penglai in the Shandong Province of China on May 7, 2006, after two days of rain.[7] Again, a water source was the catalyst behind this optical illusion.

Not every one of the so-called floating cities is the result of an optical illusion with a water source as the refractor. There are examples of floating cities that do not have a water source. And you cannot say they are due to the clouds, because clouds cannot create such mirages. Clouds may be the surface upon which the illusion is projected, much like a television screen. In my humble opinion a number of these floating cities are the direct results of Project Blue Beam. And it's important to note that Project Blue Beam could very well play a role in the rise of the Antichrist. Let me explain why.

Recorded in the Book of Exodus is the account of when God sent down a pillar of fire to block Pharaoh and his armies from killing the Israelites who were just freed from 430 years of Egyptian captivity (Exod. 14:19–24). We also know that a pillar of fire was over the Tabernacle of God by night as the children of Israel were led by God through the wilderness (Exod. 40:36–38). And we find that tongues of fire appeared over the disciples at Pentecost with the coming of the Holy Spirit (Acts 2:1–4). Even in God's creation, when the temperature is intense enough, a fire tornado can appear, usually because of a massive forest fire or buildings burning together in a concentrated area.[8]

When we look at Revelation 13:13, we find out that one of the beasts (the false prophet) will be able to call fire down from heaven. Can such an event actually happen because of occult or demonic powers? Yes, it can. When I was in the Illuminati, I personally witnessed columns of fire that were around twenty-five to thirty feet in height in a number of different ceremonies. However, there is another viable explanation for the false prophet appearing to call down fire from heaven. Since we know that Project Blue Beam is capable of creating extraordinary mirages, how much greater could those mirages be if they appeared, let's say, twenty or thirty years down the road? Think of how convincing such mirages will be that far in the future. We know that everyone will be able to see these things happen because of television and the Internet. When you add to and enhance an image with CGI (computer-generated imagery), the effect of fire descending from heaven will probably be quite overwhelming and convince everyone that such a miracle could only happen because of God. And we know that the false prophet will proclaim the Antichrist to be the new Messiah, to be God.

False signs, like false prophets and teachers, are called

"false" because they do not come from God. Their origins are from Satan or some demon. Based on some of the examples we have just gone through, I believe we can expect to see a lot more false signs in the future. How many we will see is anyone's guess, but we were warned to watch out for such events. And let's not forget we were warned of false prophets and teachers.

The apostle Peter warned us that false teachers and prophets would come among us (2 Pet. 2:1). Because of false teachings and prophecies, many Christian will easily be led astray and will end up following a person rather than Jesus Christ. Think of David Koresh, Jim Jones, and Charles Manson, just to name a few. We are also taught that the Antichrist will lie and deceive the people who are still alive during the Tribulation so convincingly that a "strong delusion" will come about (2 Thess. 2:8–12).

Remember, when we see any signs or wonders, whether they are true or not, they indicate that the next rapture is closer. And judging by what I've been witnessing over the last decade, I believe the rapture is much closer than we realize.

False signs and wonders such as the images that could be from Project Blue Beam warn us that the final rapture is close. False prophets who are date setting or prophesying things that do not line up with the Bible warn us that the final rapture is closer. False teachings such as the prosperity movement, the kundalini movement, and others indicate that the final rapture is closer. All of these false things were prophesied in the Bible and indicate that the timing of the end is near. But recently something else has been happening that is another possible sign of how close we are to the next rapture. Let's delve in and determine what we can figure out.

THE TRUMPET OF GOD

When the next rapture hits, a series of events shall occur:

> For the Lord Himself will descend from heaven with a shout, with the voice of the archangel, and with the trumpet call of God. And the dead in Christ will rise first. Then we who are alive and remain shall be caught up together with them in the clouds to meet the Lord in the air. And so we shall be forever with the Lord.
> —1 THESSALONIANS 4:16–17

First Corinthians 15:51–53 adds additional details. When the final rapture occurs, we will be changed. Our physical bodies will take on their new and vastly improved glorified state. It will happen in a moment, in the twinkling of an eye. A trumpet will sound, the dead will be raised in their new, incorruptible state; and we, the living, will also be changed at that time. The trumpet in 1 Corinthians 15 and the trumpet in 1 Thessalonians 4:16 are the same. This is the first and only time in the entire Bible when the actual trumpet of God Himself is being sounded as explained in chapter 3. And this is important to note in the study we're doing right now.

Many things we have discussed in this book thus far are reminiscent of events that already happened in the past. It seems to me that many of the events that are going on right now are reminders or foreshadowers from God. The past is repeating itself and catching up with our present, and many of the same events will also be repeated in the future. Evidence of my conjectures can be found in a strange event that has been recorded around the world in the last few years.

Trumpetlike sounds are being heard in many different places. That does tend to make me believe that we are seeing foreshadowing of an event that could happen very soon. The following are a few examples of those trumpetlike sounds that are being heard around the world. Play them for yourself and you'll very quickly be able to understand what I'm telling you right now.

One video, entitled "Very Strange Trumpet Like Sounds Heard Coming from Sky," was recorded back in January 2016.[9] This particular example has a very deep, droning sound to it. The next example was recorded in Jakarta, Indonesia, on September 11, 2015. It has a much higher, almost shrill sound at first. But then that distant, trumpetlike sound begins again. It is titled "Strange Weird 'Trumpet' Sounds from the Sky Baffle Residents of Jakarta."[10]

The next video I would ask you to watch is quite remarkable. It shows that quite a number of those trumpetlike sounds were heard in various spots around the world. The title of this video is "CMF Trumpet Sounds from Heaven (Warning From God)."[11] Did you notice how sometimes it is dark and cloudy overhead, sometimes there are scattered clouds, and sometimes the sky is clear? The atmospheric conditions were different. If the same trumpetlike sounds were heard under similar meteorological circumstances, then the explanation could lie within the meteorological realm. But since a number of trumpetlike sounds occurred with no clouds at all, weather conditions can't be considered as a viable answer.

Meteorologists have no answers for this new phenomenon that has been going on for the past few years. The military states they have no idea what is going on with trumpetlike sounds. I doubt it could be HAARP (the US government's High Frequency Active Auroral Research Program) because that instrument could not cause the variable resonant sounds we all heard. They were too varied in their pitch.

I believe we could be looking at another pre-sign from God. At this point it's the only thing that makes sense. I also believe that this could very well indicate that we are much further along on the prophetic timeline than many might think.

Trumpetlike sounds are being heard around the world. We were warned to look for signs and wonders in heaven before the next rapture. I believe this is what we are witnessing now—signs of the imminent appearance of Jesus Christ in the clouds when we will be raptured up to Him. Prepare yourselves, everyone. All signs are pointing to God preparing to send Jesus Christ to us very soon, and according to the prophecies, that time will be within our generation. So get ready, because the best is yet to come.

Where do all the things that we just discussed put us on the prophetic timeline? If you recall, our starting point was when Israel became a sovereign nation back in 1948. When we added the biblical measurement of a generation as seventy to eighty years, we ended up between 2018 and 2028, with another possible end date of 2068 based on a 120-year generation. So the next rapture could occur somewhere between 2018 and 2068. Remember, this is only a possibility and not a certainty. We are not date setting here; we are running the biblical numbers and comparing them to what the Scriptures teach us of the events that shall precede the next rapture. We are looking at what the possibilities could be and nothing more. Please remember that God alone knows the exact time when the next and final rapture will occur.

We are the children of the Most High God. We are directly, spiritually connected to the Creator of everything. Because we have such a unique and most blessed connection, we can sense something is in the prophetic air. Something is about to burst forth on the prophetic scene. It's as if we can feel something approaching, something imminent, something that can't be held back, and if all the prophetic indications are correct, it could very well be the final rapture. And I for one cannot wait until I go home.

Part III
HOPE FOR THE UNSAVED
(THE FUTURE)

Chapter 10
WITNESSING TO THOSE LIVING AFTER THE RAPTURE (A LETTER IN A BOTTLE)

W E ARE NOW turning our attention to the people who will be living in the future during the Tribulation—the seven-year period during which the Antichrist will arise, set up his new world order, and quite literally become the world dictator described in the Book of Revelation and other places in the Holy Bible. Though I won't be able to examine every jot and tittle due to space restraints, we will cover the major events of the Tribulation and the prophecies surrounding them. Having said all that, let's turn our attention now to the future and those who will be enduring the Tribulation.

TO THOSE IN THE FUTURE: SOMETHING JUST HAPPENED

Something happened—something so frightening and mysterious, it defies explanation. It might have happened as you were walking down the street and passing by multitudes of strangers. It might have happened as you were speaking face-to-face with a friend or a colleague. It might have happened as you were having a conversation with someone on your cell phone. It might have even happened while you were asleep. Regardless of what you were doing when it actually happened, all of a sudden tens of millions, if not hundreds of millions of people around the world suddenly vanished. They quite literally just vanished! And now you're stuck wondering what happened.

My name is Doc Marquis, and I'm sending you this message, this letter in a bottle from the past, in order to explain to you what is going on in the day and age you're living in. You are in a situation right now that is both frightening and most dire. And unfortunately it's only going to get worse. However, you are not without hope! There is a ray of sunshine, a sure anchor that you'll be able to hold on to that I will explain to you as we go through the rest of this book. I earnestly pray that you read this entire book from beginning to end, because there are eternal consequences to the decisions you make now. And I do mean *eternal* consequences. But for now let's move on so I can begin to explain to you what happened to all those people who suddenly vanished, and what you can expect to happen in your future. As I explain everything to you, I will be using a number of sources, but I will primarily be using the Bible. I will also use certain other sources as we move along.

WHAT HAPPENED?

Your friends and possibly your family members vanished. Old people in retirement homes suddenly disappeared. Babies in hospital nurseries or family homes are now gone. Even little children seem to be missing without a trace. What happened?

In the Christian world there is an event known as the rapture. Without getting in too deep here, the Bible prophesied that one day Jesus Christ would return for those who became Christians. And by Christians, I mean true, born-again, sold-out people who wanted to live their lives according to the way Jesus Christ taught us to live and not by the way mankind taught us to live through their created religions. You see, Christianity is not a religion—it never has been and never will be. Christianity is the way Jesus Christ taught us to live. In essence, it's a lifestyle.

Periodically I will be quoting the Bible to explain to you precisely what the Word of God has to say. The Bible is the Word of God. I believe the Bible will be outlawed in your day and age and possessing one will probably be punished by imprisonment or even death. Since I believe you won't have a Bible at hand, I will be quoting it for you to show you what God has to say. Now, back to the rapture.

In 1 Thessalonians 4:16–18 the Bible says:

> For the Lord Himself will descend from heaven with a shout, with the voice of the archangel, and with the trumpet call of God. And the dead in Christ will rise first. Then we who are alive and remain shall be caught up together with them in the clouds to meet the Lord in the air. And so we shall be forever with the Lord. Therefore comfort one another with these words.

As promised, Jesus Christ appeared in the clouds overhead and called all of His born-again children off this planet and took them to heaven. And as you read along in this book, you will find that the Lord took His children with Him to heaven for seven years and then they will all return. But we will further delve into these events as we move along.

Allow me to illustrate the event we just discussed. There

is a painting, found at http://www.armageddonbooks.com /print.html, that in my opinion best illustrates the rapture. At the very top of the painting we see a figure in the middle that represents Jesus Christ appearing in the clouds. Toward the bottom of the painting, numerous figures dressed in white robes are beginning to rise toward the Lord.[1] These are the born-again Christians for whom the Lord came back to take them to heaven. This is only part of what happened during the rapture you missed out on.

Aside from the Lord appearing in the clouds, many other things can be seen in this drawing:

- On the left side of the painting toward the middle, there is a plane that crashed into a building, and a number of white-clothed individuals are rising toward the clouds.

- On the bottom of the painting, all the way to the right, there is a graveyard with white-clothed individuals rising out of their graves toward the Lord Jesus Christ.

- At the bottom in the middle there is a yellow van that crashed into a guardrail, and two individuals dressed in white are rising up toward the Lord.

- Throughout the painting there are other accidents that occurred.

The reason those things occurred is because people were immediately called up to meet Jesus Christ in the clouds when the rapture occurred:

- The plane crashed because there was no more pilot.

- The people in their graves rose because the Bible teaches us that the dead in Christ (born-again Christians who died before the rapture) will rise.

- The yellow van hit the guardrail because there was no one left to drive the van.

- Other accidents occurred because of vehicles that were suddenly without drivers.

This next Bible passage that we'll examine is found in 1 Corinthians 15:51–52:

> Listen, I tell you a mystery: We shall not all sleep, but we shall all be changed. In a moment, in the twinkling of an eye, at the last trumpet, for the trumpet will sound, the dead will be raised incorruptible, and we shall be changed.

If you remember, the previous verses we looked at in 1 Thessalonians 4 confirmed that "the dead in Christ" would rise—they would rise first, and then all the born-again Christians alive at the moment of the rapture would rise off the earth next. These events happened so quickly that by the time you could blink your eye, it was all over with. Every born-again Christian, dead or alive, has risen off the earth and is now with Jesus Christ in heaven.

You might be saying, "Well, that's fine and dandy. But what about me? What's going to happen next? Can I still be saved?"

To begin, let me reassure you right now that you are not

without hope! You can still be saved right now, but you will meet Jesus Christ later on. Again, this is one of those things I will explain to you as we move along. We will explore what will happen next, because there are many things that will happen to you and everyone else left on the earth.

What Does It Mean
to Be Born Again?

Let me explain what it means to be saved, or to become a born-again Christian. As I've already stated, for a true believer in Christ, Christianity is not a religion but a way of life—the way of life Christ instructed us to follow through His holy words found in the Bible. Being a born-again Christian is a learning and growing process that will continue for the rest of your life. You learn things from the Word of God, you try to follow His Word as well as you can, and when you mess up or sin, you get back on your feet, brush yourself off, and try again. And perhaps the next time you won't fall for that sin again.

One of the most important things I can teach you right now is that becoming a born-again Christian does not make you perfect. It doesn't make you any better than anyone else. True Christianity is when you commit your entire life to Jesus Christ, and at the same time you try to stop doing things your way and start doing things God's way. And God's way of doing things can be found in His own words in the Bible. If you're fortunate, there may also be a Bible lying around somewhere wherever you found this book, so look for it. But also remember, if you can't find a Bible, I will be quoting all the verses that are used for this part of the book.

A true born-again Christian will always admit that he or she has sinned. Now sin in its simplest definition is when you do something that is against the will of God. Would God ever do something He considers wrong? The answer obviously is no. A born-again Christian strives to adhere to the same standard. However, because we are not perfect like God, and because we are still human, we do sin. And when we do sin, we go to God in prayer, admit it to Him, and try not to do that sin again.

So now you know what sin is, and you also know what being a true born-again Christian is all about. The next thing you need to learn is what salvation is and how you get saved.

In a nutshell salvation means that you commit yourself to doing things God's way. You realize that you can't live the best possible life or serve Jesus Christ to your fullest on your own. You need Jesus; you can't do it without Him. And as stated before, getting saved does not make you perfect. It does mean that you're going to try to do things His way to the best of your ability for the rest of your life.

The most important thing I can teach you is how to get saved. As always, when looking for answers, we will delve straight into the Holy Bible. So let's take the first steps that, Lord willing, will get you saved right now.

There are four very easy steps that I show everyone who wants to get saved. God purposely made salvation easy to acquire because He truly does love you and wants you to eventually join Him in heaven.

STEP ONE

The first step in getting saved is asking yourself if you have ever sinned in your life.

The next passage of the Bible we will look at is Romans 3:10:

> There is none righteous, no, not one.

When this verse speaks of no one being righteous, it means that you are not innocent—you have committed sin in your life. And not just you—everyone has sinned! I sinned, you sinned, and everyone else we can think of sinned.

Romans 3:23 reads:

> For all have sinned and come short of the glory of God.

This verse clearly points out that everyone has sinned. And if you'll recall, sin is doing anything outside of the will of God. So if you've ever done anything you know God would not approve of, then you've sinned.

Sin has a price, a very heavy price. Romans 6:23 teaches us:

> For the wages of sin is death, but the gift of God is eternal life through Jesus Christ our Lord.

In the first part of the verse the word *wages* means "a payment." In other words, the payment of sin is death. And death is the place known as hell. So if you sin, then the price for that sin has to be paid in hell, and that would be a most just punishment. However, the good news is that the verse doesn't end there. It continues by saying, "but the gift of God is eternal life through Jesus Christ our Lord." The most incredible thing about this verse is that you have a way of avoiding paying for all of your sins in hell. The second half of this verse teaches us three critical things:

- God has a gift for us.

- That gift is eternal life, where we don't end
  up in hell.

- We get this gift through Jesus Christ.

So step one in learning how to become a born-again Christian is asking yourself if you have ever sinned. The answer is yes. Let's take a moment to review what you just learned:

- You have sinned.

- The punishment for sin is hell.

- God provided a way out so you don't have to
  pay for all your sins in hell.

- The way out God provided is the gift known
  as eternal salvation; you get this gift through
  Jesus Christ.

STEP TWO

Step two in getting saved and becoming a born-again Christian is realizing that you could never pay for your sins but that Jesus Christ paid for all of them by dying on the cross for you and me. Because Jesus never sinned, He was able to pay the price for our sins through His death on the cross. Second Corinthians 5:21 tells us:

> God made [Jesus] who knew no sin to be sin for
> us, that we might become the righteousness of God
> in Him.

In other words, Jesus took our sin away and gave us His righteousness when He died on the cross. But even though Jesus died in our place, He didn't stay dead. He rose from the dead, victorious over the power of sin and death. The Bible tells us in 1 Corinthians 15:3–4:

> Christ died for our sins according to the Scriptures, was buried, [and] rose again the third day according to the Scriptures.

We also learn from 1 Corinthians 15:24–26 that:

> [Jesus] will deliver up the kingdom to God the Father, when He puts an end to all rule and all authority and power. For He will reign until He has put all enemies under His feet. The last enemy that will be destroyed is death.

So Jesus triumphed over all enemies, including death, through His death on the cross and His resurrection (when He rose from the dead) three days later. The Bible also tells us why Jesus Christ was willing to die on the cross and pay for our sins. John 3:16 reads:

> For God so loved the world that He gave His only begotten Son, that whoever believes in Him should not perish, but have eternal life.

God loved you and me so much that He was willing to send His own Son, Jesus Christ (who is God in physical form), to die on the cross and pay for all of our sins so we would not have to spend eternity in hell. Instead, as you just read, God wants to give us eternal life. I don't know about you, but that's what I call love!

When I was alive (before the rapture), there was a ridiculous belief that anyone could work their way into heaven. In other words, if your good deeds outweighed your bad deeds, you could go straight to heaven. That is not what the Bible teaches us. Ephesians 2:8–9 reads as follows:

> For by grace you have been saved through faith, and this is not of yourselves. It is the gift of God, not of works, so that no one should boast.

Notice how the verses tell us that we are saved through faith. That faith, as you will soon learn, is placed in what Jesus Christ was willing to do for us. The end result of faith is getting saved, receiving "the gift of God," which, as you already learned, is the gift of eternal salvation.

These verses also teach us that we cannot receive the gift of God through works: "It is the gift of God, not of works." So these verses are saying that we receive eternal salvation by accepting the gift of eternal salvation through God and that we cannot work for it. It's very straightforward. If you want to get to heaven, you can't work for it. You have to accept the gift of eternal salvation through God. You need to accept His payment, His sacrifice for your sins.

In step two of how to get saved, we read through God's Word that:

- God loves us so much that He gave up His own Son, Jesus Christ, who never sinned, to die on the cross to pay for all our sins and to impart His righteousness to us.

- Jesus died on the cross, but He didn't stay dead. He rose from the dead and triumphed over sin and death.

- Jesus died on the cross because He knew we couldn't pay for all of our own sins and work our way into heaven.

- By accepting what Jesus Christ did for us on the cross, we receive the gift of eternal salvation.

Thus far this is pretty easy stuff to understand, and it's going to remain this easy because God wanted it to be that way. God wanted salvation to be so easy to acquire that everyone could get it if they wanted to. That's how much He loves us.

Step Three

Step three of how to get saved is repenting of your sins. By *repenting*, I don't mean you're going to suddenly turn into some Holy Roller or suddenly never ever sin again in your life. To *repent* means to try to stop sinning, to turn from your sin, and to stop doing things your way and start doing things God's way. You learn about doing things God's way by reading the Bible and finding out what it is He wants of you. As I stated before, I am convinced that the Bible is going to be outlawed in your time period. If it's not, then God be praised because you can still very easily learn how God wants you to live and act by reading the Bible. However, if I'm correct, the Bible will be outlawed and possession of one will be punishable by death. Be that as it may, I am convinced that in whatever home, bookstore, or church building you found this book, you'll also find a Bible somewhere. I believe this because a born-again Christian either lived there, sold books there, or worshipped there before the rapture hit. Therefore, search that place and try to find a Bible there. Lord willing, you'll find one before all of them are destroyed.

The Bible tells us in Mark 1:15:

> The time is fulfilled, and the kingdom of God is at hand. Repent and believe the gospel.

Let me explain a couple of things here before we get into verse 15. First of all, if you read Mark 1:15 from a Bible, in many versions the words will be in red. Whenever you see any words in red letters, those words were spoken by Christ Himself. So in Mark 1:15, Jesus Christ is speaking. Second, the word *gospel* means "good news" or "good message." The good news is that Jesus died in your place so you don't have to pay the penalty for your own sin. Knowing these things, verse 15 is teaching us three things:

- The kingdom of God is close.

- Christ is asking you, as He asked people back when He walked the earth, to repent of your sins, to turn from your sin.

- Christ is asking you, as He asked people back when He walked the earth, to believe in the good news He has for you.

So the third step in getting saved is to repent and believe the good news that your sin has been paid for by Jesus.

STEP FOUR

Now, the fourth and final step in getting saved is accepting the gift of eternal salvation that Jesus Christ wants to give you this very second. Right now Jesus wants to give you His gift of everlasting salvation if you're willing to accept it.

In the Bible, Romans 10:9 reads as follows:

> If you confess with your mouth Jesus is Lord, and believe in your heart that God has raised Him from the dead, you will be saved.

This is further emphasized in Romans 10:13, where it reads:

> Everyone who calls on the name of the Lord shall be saved.

These two verses teach us that if we believe in our hearts that Jesus Christ was resurrected from the dead and acknowledge that fact with our spoken words by calling upon Jesus Christ to save us, then we are saved. It's that easy. Believe that Christ died for your sins and that He arose from the dead, and you will be saved.

TODAY IS THE DAY OF SALVATION

We have reviewed the four steps, and now it is time to get you that gift of everlasting salvation. The Bible tells us in 2 Corinthians 6:2:

> Now is the day of salvation.

That means the time to get saved is now, today, right this moment. Don't put it off until tomorrow, because you don't know what tomorrow may hold. Today is the day of salvation.

Right now I'm going to ask you four easy questions based upon the four steps to salvation.

1. Have you ever sinned in your life? I know that I, and everyone else I knew when I was alive, sinned. So can you admit to God right now that you have sinned? Pretend God is standing in front of you right now and asking you this question: Have you ever sinned in your life? A simple "yes" or "no" is all that is required. The answer is quite simple: "Yes, I have sinned." Once you have admitted that, let's move on.

2. Do you believe that Jesus Christ died on the cross and was resurrected to pay for all your sins so that one day you could join Him in heaven? Do you believe Jesus Christ did all of this for you? Again, a "yes" or "no" is all that God is looking for right now. Hopefully you just said, "Yes."

3. Are you willing to repent of your sins? In other words, are you willing to stop doing things your way and start doing things God's way? If you want to do things God's way, please say, "Yes."

4. Are you willing to accept the gift of everlasting salvation from Jesus Christ and allow Him to be your personal Lord and Savior? Again, please say either "yes" or "no."

If you just said "yes" to all four of my questions, we're ready to get you that gift of eternal salvation right now. Here's what we're going to do. I'm going to open us up with a prayer, which you will read, and present you to God. Once I have done that, you are going to say a prayer. So from the past, here is my prayer to God as I present you before Him. Read this prayer carefully and thoughtfully:

Dear heavenly Father, I thank You for allowing me to once again present to You another person who wants to accept Your gift of eternal salvation. Please listen to his or her heart, Father, as we go through this sinner's prayer.

Now it's your turn to pray to God. Say these words out loud now and believe them within your heart so that you can get saved:

Dear heavenly Father, I admit that I am a sinner. And because I am a sinner, I do deserve the punishment of hell. But I believe that Jesus Christ died on the cross and paid for all of my sins, that He was resurrected from the dead, and that He did all these things for me so that one day I could join Him in heaven. I repent of my sins and will try my best to do things Your way. I accept Your gift of eternal salvation right now and claim it as my own. I also ask You, Lord, to come into my heart right now and be my personal Lord and Savior for the rest of my life. I ask all these things of You right now and

thank You for all of these things in Jesus's most
precious and holy name. Amen.

Let me be the first to say, "Welcome to the family of
God." If you meant every single word of that prayer you
just prayed, then you are saved. You are now a child of
the Most High God and one day will be with Him as I am
with Him right now. Many people have told me that when
they got saved, it felt as if a great weight was suddenly
taken off their shoulders. Others have told me they felt a
tingly sensation or that they felt a little bit light-headed
after they prayed. Sometimes these things happen, sometimes they don't. In any case, because you admitted you
are a sinner who needs Jesus Christ and called out to Him
to save you, you are now saved!

The question that you and I need to go through now
is, what happens next? That's a bit of a tough question,
because I don't know at what point during the Tribulation
you are right now. I know that you are living during the
Tribulation, but because the Tribulation will last for seven
years, you could be anywhere in that time period right
now. So in order to help you in the best way that I can,
you and I are going to be reading through much of the
last book in the Bible, the Book of Revelation. This last
book of the Bible will give us the best idea of where you
are during the Tribulation time period and what you can
expect to happen during that period of time. Therefore,
we are going to pretend that the rapture just happened a
couple of minutes ago and all of those people just vanished. As we go through the Book of Revelation, we are
going to learn what you can expect to happen in your life
and what you can do about it.

Chapter 11
THE BEGINNING OF THE END

As WE GO through the Book of Revelation, you need to understand one important fact: I don't know everything. No one does except for God. Since the Book of Revelation deals mainly with prophecy about what was still the future when I was alive, all I can do is describe the things you can expect to happen in the best way I can. Lord willing, I will be able to help guide you through those events. Remember, I am not perfect, so I may not get everything right. But hopefully and prayerfully I will be able to get most things correct and be of some service to you as you go through the Tribulation. Before we begin looking into the prophecies of the events that are transpiring during your day and age, let me give you the background to the Book of Revelation. Then we'll move on.

JOHN AND THE ISLE OF PATMOS

In AD 95 Domitian was the reigning emperor of the Roman Empire. He had been the emperor for fourteen years, and he ruled with an iron fist. Domitian was also a megalomaniac. He even proclaimed himself to be a living god, insisting on being addressed as "master and god." The Roman emperors who ruled before Domitian believed that they would become gods when they died, but Domitian couldn't wait. His cruelty and megalomania caused problems with the Roman Senate.[1]

Revelation 1:1 introduces the book and tells us who authored it:

> The Revelation of Jesus Christ, which God gave to Him to show to His servants things which must soon take place. He sent and signified it by His angel to His servant John.

In short, God the Father gave the Book of Revelation to Jesus Christ (God the Son), who gave it to an angel, who gave it to the apostle John. At the time when he wrote the Book of Revelation, the apostle John was a convict. It's true! In AD 95, at around ninety-five years of age, John committed a crime that actually garnered the attention of Emperor Domitian in a very dangerous way.

At this time in history Roman society was flooded with a variety of gods that made up its pantheon. The people were so steeped in this polytheistic society that many years earlier the apostle Paul saw an altar "TO THE UNKNOWN GOD" (Acts 17:23). This altar was dedicated to any god that the Romans might have forgotten about or not known about. It may sound ridiculous, but it is true.

So what was the great and terrible crime that the apostle John was guilty of? Revelation 1:9 gives us the answer:

> I, John, both your brother and companion in the tribulation and kingdom and patience of Jesus Christ, was on the isle that is called Patmos on account of the word of God and the testimony of Jesus Christ.

So John's crime was that he preached that there is but one God and Jesus Christ was that one God in physical form. That was one of the worst crimes you could have committed back then. To proclaim that there was only one God instead of the many gods of the Roman culture was to go against the societal grain. What made this crime even worse was the fact that Domitian believed himself to be a living god, and John's preaching directly refuted Domitian's status as a god. Domitian was also paranoid, and he saw John as a direct threat to his authority and his position as a so-called god. As a result, John was exiled to Patmos, where he was given the visions found in the Book of Revelation.

The Isle of Patmos is very much like Alcatraz Island in the middle of San Francisco Bay. It is an island in the Aegean Sea where the Roman Empire had a prison. John was exiled to Patmos as punishment for his crime. Due to his advanced age, John would not have been expected to do hard labor. Remember, he was around ninety-five years old at the time. More than likely, because he could read and write, John probably kept the records of supplies that came in and out of Patmos and any other records related to the prison's activities.

In September of AD 96 Domitian was assassinated and the Roman Senate replaced him with Emperor Nerva. As a result of this exchange of power, John and many of the prisoners on Patmos received pardons and were set free.

THE OUTLINE OF REVELATION

Now that you have the background to the Book of Revelation, we are going to get right into the Book and develop a timeline so you can try to determine where in the Tribulation you are right now.

When the apostle John received the prophecies of the Book of Revelation, he was also given the outline of the book. In Revelation 1:19 Jesus Christ told John:

> Write the things which you have seen, and the things which are, and the things which will take place after this.

So the outline of the Book of Revelation is easy and goes as follows:

- The things which you have seen—the things that John was told in chapter 1 of the Book of Revelation; John's immediate past

- The things which are—chapters 2 and 3 of the Book of Revelation; what John witnessed in his present

- The things which will take place after this— chapters 4 to 22 of the Book of Revelation, the prophecies of the future; what you are living through right now

This is the divine outline of the Book of Revelation. It includes the past, the present, and the future.

THE SEVEN CHURCH AGES

You are living during the Tribulation period as previously revealed. The reason you are living during this time period is because you did not get saved before the rapture—you did not accept Jesus's gift of eternal salvation and become a born-again Christian. Sometime in your life you were given an opportunity to get saved, but for some reason you didn't. In my experience some excuses people gave me when I witnessed to them were, "I don't have the time to listen to you right now," "I'll accept Jesus Christ later on," "I don't want to hear it," "I just don't believe the Bible," and so on. Perhaps you don't remember when you had the opportunity to get saved. Perhaps you used one of those common excuses. No matter the circumstance or reason, you rejected Jesus's gift of eternal salvation. However, you may not be the only one to blame for your present state of existence. So often the reason a person does not get saved is because a demon was working to prevent it. This may sound strange to you at first, but it is the truth. Satan, who has already been found guilty and will be condemned in the near future, wants to destroy as many people as he can. Satan tries to prevent as many people as he can from going to heaven to be with God. This is the ultimate act of vindictiveness. Since he has already been condemned, Satan wants to take as many people down with him as possible. However, there is also someone else responsible for your present plight, and once we have gone through the seven church ages, I will reveal this other culprit to you.

The seven churches spoken of and explained in Revelation 2 and 3 were seven physical churches that were established in various parts of the Roman Empire when the apostle John was alive. The seven churches were Ephesus, Smyrna, Pergamum, Thyatira, Sardis, Philadelphia, and Laodicea. However, the seven churches also symbolically represent the seven church ages of Christianity. Let me break it down for you:

- Ephesus: AD 30–AD 100

- Smyrna: AD 100–AD 312

- Pergamum: AD 312–AD 600

- Thyatira: AD 600–AD 1517

- Sardis: AD 1517–AD 1750

- Philadelphia: AD 1750–AD 1920

- Laodicea: AD 1920–rapture

Notice that the age of Ephesus began in AD 30, the year we believe Jesus Christ was crucified and then resurrected. From AD 30 all the way up to when the rapture happened (around two thousand years) is the whole of the history of Christianity. During the two thousand years of the history of Christianity, there were seven major periods of time, or ages, that defined and explained what was going on within the Christian church. Once we go through those seven church ages, we will be able to identify the third person who may have been responsible for your rejection of Christ prior to the rapture. That being said, let's briefly take a look at those seven church ages.

THE CHURCH OF EPHESUS (AD 30–AD 100)

I will now describe to you the features that identified the character of each of the seven churches (and church ages), beginning with Ephesus. Each of the churches received a commendation, a reproof or correction, counsel or words of advice, and encouragement. The only exceptions were Laodicea, which received no commendation, and Smyrna and Philadelphia, which received no reproof. We'll get into that soon enough, but for now let's examine the first church age, Ephesus. Jesus Christ's description of the church age of Ephesus is found in Revelation 2:1–7:

> To the angel of the church of Ephesus write:
> He who holds the seven stars in His right hand, who walks in the midst of the seven golden candlesticks, says these things: I know your works, your labor and your patience, and that you cannot bear those who are evil. And you have tested those who say they are apostles, but are not, and have found them to be liars. You have endured, and have been patient, and for My name's sake have labored and have not grown weary.
> But I have something against you, that you have abandoned the love you had at first. Remember therefore from where you have fallen. Repent, and do the works you did at first, or else I will come to you quickly and remove your candlestick from its place, unless you repent. But this you have: You hate the works of the Nicolaitans, which I also hate.
> He who has an ear, let him hear what the Spirit says to the churches. To him who overcomes I will give permission to eat of the tree of life, which is in the midst of the Paradise of God.

Let's take a look at the four elements found in the description of each church age.

- **Commendation**—"I know your works,
  your labor and your patience, and that you
  cannot bear those who are evil. And you
  have tested those who say they are apostles,

but are not, and have found them to be liars.
You have endured, and have been patient,
and for My name's sake have labored and
have not grown weary.... You hate the works
of the Nicolaitans."

- **Reproof**—"You have abandoned the love
  you had at first."

- **Counsel**—"Remember therefore from where
  you have fallen. Repent, and do the works
  you did at first."

- **Encouragement**—"To him who overcomes
  I will give permission to eat of the tree of
  life, which is in the midst of the Paradise
  of God."

The church (age) of Ephesus received a number of com-
mendations from the Lord. They did good works, they
hated evil, they never stopped doing the Lord's work, and
so forth. This is what the earliest days of Christianity were
all about. People were excited to be saved, they learned the
teachings of Jesus Christ, and they lived their lives by the
Lord's teachings. But something happened within those
seventy years that caused a lot of early Christians to back-
slide (to move away from things that are good in the eyes
of God), and this is why they also received a reproof from
the Lord.

The church of Ephesus also received counsel from the
Lord. He told them to remember where they had fallen
from. Jesus was advising them to remember their begin-
nings, which were strongly rooted in the way of life about
which He had instructed them. The Lord also told them

to repent, to stop doing things their way and get back to doing things His way.

The good Lord did not just leave those early Christians hanging with a bad report card. He also had a word of encouragement for them. The Lord told them there was a special place for those who overcame, who corrected themselves. They would be able to enter the center of God's paradise and eat of the tree of life. This would be quite a reward for those who obeyed the instructions of the Lord.

As you should be able to tell by now, the church of Ephesus had its good points and its bad points. Just like the Christians who lived during the church age of Ephesus, choose not to be like everyone else living in the world. Even during the time of tribulation you're living through right now, hold strong to your Christian faith. Be a light to the world so everyone can see there is a better way of living than trying to be a part of the Antichrist's system (Matt. 5:14–16). Even though you will face many diffi-cult events, Jesus Christ promised that if you endure to the end (in this case to the end of the Tribulation or your life), you will eat of the tree of life found in the Paradise of God. So hang in there! Commit your life and faith to Jesus Christ, who will always be there for you, no matter the circumstances.

THE CHURCH OF SMYRNA
(AD 100–AD 312)

By the time the Christian church reached this period of time, they had remembered from where they had fallen and returned to their first love. The early Christian church became a fire for the Lord that could not be stopped no matter how much persecution they endured. Let's see what the Bible records about the church at this period of time in Revelation 2:8–11:

> To the angel of the church in Smyrna write:
> The First and the Last, who was dead and came to life, says these things: I know your works and tribulation and poverty (but you are rich). And I know the blasphemy of those who say they are Jews and are not, but are a synagogue of Satan. Do not fear any of those things which you are about to suffer. Look, the devil is about to throw some of you into prison, that you may be tried, and you will have tribulation for ten days. Be faithful unto death, and I will give you the crown of life.
> He who has an ear, let him hear what the Spirit says to the churches. He who overcomes shall not be hurt by the second death.

This is the account of the church of Smyrna. Let's take a look at the four elements in the Lord's description of this church age.

- **Commendation**—"I know your works and tribulation and poverty (but you are rich)."

- **Reproof**—There is not one word of correction.

- **Counsel**—"Do not fear any of those things which you are about to suffer.... Be faithful unto death."

- **Encouragement**—"I will give you the crown of life...He who overcomes shall not be hurt by the second death."

The first age of Christianity was when the early church began to learn how to grow. It was like a baby learning to walk. By the second age of the church, the church age of Smyrna, the church had learned not just to walk but to run. It was on fire for the Lord! The Word of Christ began to spread throughout the Roman world like a forest fire. The Lord gave the church a commendation for their works and for the persecution they faced. They were materially poor, but they were spiritually rich. Because the church was doing the right things at this point, the Lord did not need to correct them about anything. This was one of only two times in church history that the church did not receive a reproof or a correction from the Lord.

The Lord also counseled His people to "not fear any of those things which you are about to suffer" and to "be faithful unto death." You are living through the worst time in human history, during which the Antichrist will have full reign over the earth and the judgments from God will severely punish the earth. Do not be afraid of these things! Easier said than done, I know. However, remember that no matter what may happen, you are a child of God as a born-again believer. Your position in God's family is fixed and can never be altered. No matter what happens, you will eventually join Him in heaven. So when the tough times hit, remember who you are in God's family and where you will eventually end up.

Always try to remain faithful to God to the best of your ability. You may endure severe persecution, torture, or martyrdom. In your day and age these are going to be very real events. No matter what may happen, stand your ground and be faithful to God. Never deny Him, never lose faith in Him, and never let go of Him. God will always be with you through it all.

Because the good Lord knew that His children were about to go through a horrible time of persecution, He sent them a word of encouragement. He warned them that the devil would throw some of them into prison and they would have tribulation (or be persecuted) for ten days.

Before going any further with this topic, I need to explain something important to you. The Book of Revelation was written about things John personally saw and witnessed in heaven. Much of what John saw, he had never been exposed to. John saw things from our time that he would not have understood. So John used a lot of symbolism to describe what he saw.

From this particular passage in the Bible we learn that many Christians living during the second church age (our brothers and sisters in the Lord) would be thrown into prison because they held their ground and spread Christianity throughout the whole of the Roman Empire. Our brothers and sisters back then knew the law, and they knew what Rome would do to them for proclaiming the one true God. But the threat of prison and possible execution did not stop them. They held firm to their faith and took a stand for Christ.

We also learn from these verses that these particular Christians would face tribulation for ten days. The "ten days" is one of the symbols you and I need to decipher so we can understand the context of what we read in this passage. Symbolically the ten days are the ten Roman emperors who persecuted the church. Here is a list of the emperors with examples of how Christians faced persecution during their reigns:

1. Emperor Nero (AD 54–AD 68)—The apostle Paul was beheaded, and the apostle Peter was crucified upside down. Nero was known for using Christians as human torches to light his parties.

2. Emperor Domitian (AD 81–AD 96)—The apostle John was boiled in oil and exiled to Patmos. Simeon, the bishop of Jerusalem, was crucified.

3. Emperor Trajan (AD 98–AD 117)—The famous early Christian writer Ignatius was martyred by being devoured by lions at the Colosseum.

4. Emperor Marcus Aurelius (AD 161–AD 180)—Justin Martyr, a second-century apologist, was beheaded along with his disciples.

5. Emperor Septimius Severus (AD 193–AD 211)—Christian noblewoman Perpetua was arrested, imprisoned, and executed.

6. Emperor Maximinus I (AD 235–AD 238)—Maximinus commanded that the rulers of churches be put to death.

7. Emperor Trajan Decius (AD 249–AD 251)—Fabian, the bishop of Rome, was martyred.

8. Emperor Valerian (AD 253–AD 260)—
   Stephen, the bishop of Rome, was beheaded.

9. Emperor Aurelian (AD 270–AD 275)—
   Felix, the bishop of Rome, was reportedly
   beheaded.

10. Emperor Diocletian (AD 284–AD 305)—
    Edicts were issued ordering the destruction
    of Christian church buildings and sacred
    writings, the arrest of all clergy, and the
    death of all Christians who refused to sacri-
    fice to the empire.

The ten Roman emperors are the ten days of persecution or tribulation the Christian church would face. This
is what I mean when I speak of symbolism. As I stated
before, symbolism can be tricky to discern properly, which
is why I have been studying the Book of Revelation for
almost forty years now.

Going back to the church of Smyrna, Jesus Christ did
leave them with some encouragement. He stated that those
who overcome would not be hurt by the second death.

Born-again Christians symbolically go through a
death. That death is a spiritual death—we die to our old
nature (our sinful, unsaved self) and become a new person
through Jesus Christ when we get saved (become a born-
again Christian). Because of the gift of eternal salvation,
we no longer have to concern ourselves with our final destination. As born-again children of God, we enter heaven
when we die.

I explained this so you can more easily understand what
the second death is. The second death refers to the final

judgment, when Jesus Christ will judge all the unsaved and condemn them to eternity in the lake of fire. Many people think that hell is the final destination if you don't go to heaven. That is incorrect. Hell is actually a temporary stop where the unsaved will remain until the final judgment. The lake of fire is the final destination for those who are not saved. It breaks my heart to think about all the people who will have to endure eternity without being in the presence of Jesus Christ, but their actions dictated the consequences. You and I (if you get saved before the end of the Tribulation) won't have to face such an eternity. Once you became a born-again Christian by getting saved through Jesus Christ, your eternity was secured— you will spend all of eternity in heaven with Jesus Christ. I am truly grateful for this because it means that one day we will enjoy the company of Jesus Christ together. Now that's an eternity to look forward to.

THE CHURCH OF PERGAMUM
(AD 312–AD 600)

The third church age, the age of Pergamum, is described by Jesus in Revelation 2:12–17:

> To the angel of the church in Pergamum write:
> He who has the sharp two-edged sword says these things: I know your works and where you live, where Satan's throne is. Yet you hold firmly to My name, and did not deny My faith even in the days of Antipas, My faithful martyr, who was killed among you, where Satan dwells.
> But I have a few things against you: You have there those who hold the teaching of Balaam, who

taught Balak to cast a stumbling block before the children of Israel, to eat things sacrificed to idols and to commit sexual immorality. So you also have those who hold the teaching of the Nicolaitans. Repent, or else I will come to you quickly and will war against them with the sword of My mouth.

He who has an ear, let him hear what the Spirit says to the churches. To him who overcomes I will give the hidden manna to eat. And I will give him a white stone, and on the stone a new name written, which no one knows except he who receives it.

Let's take a look at the four elements found in the description of the church age of Pergamum.

- **Commendation**—"You hold firmly to My name, and did not deny My faith even in the days of Antipas, My faithful martyr, who was killed among you."

- **Reproof**—"You have there those who hold the teaching of Balaam....So you also have those who hold the teaching of the Nicolaitans."

- **Counsel**—"Repent."

- **Encouragement**—"To him who overcomes I will give the hidden manna to eat. And I will give him a white stone, and on the stone a new name written, which no one knows except he who receives it."

Diocletian, the last of the ten emperors representing the ten days of tribulation, abdicated the throne of Rome in AD 305. Two main people contended for control of the Roman Empire: Constantine and Galerius. After Galerius's death in 311, Maxentius was Constantine's main adversary. On October 27, 312, the day before the Battle of Milvian Bridge, Constantine had a vision of a cross with the words "*In hoc signo vinces* [In this sign conquer]." Constantine directed his soldiers to put the symbol of Christ on their shields, and they were victorious in the battle against the armies of Maxentius the next day.[2]

There was a succession of battles until AD 324, when Constantine secured his position as the sole emperor of the Roman Empire, but the Battle of Milvian Bridge forever changed Constantine's religious beliefs because he gave the credit for the victory to the Christian God. In AD 313 Constantine issued the famous "Edict of Milan," which read in part that "no one whatsoever should be denied the opportunity to give his heart to the observance of the Christian religion" and "any one of these who wishes to observe Christian religion may do so freely and openly, without molestation."[3] Because of Constantine's edict, Christians could no longer be burned at the stake, fed to the lions, or tortured for their faith.

Constantine, before his so-called conversion to Christianity, was a practicing pagan like most Roman citizens of that day and age. In AD 325, the year after he secured the throne of the Roman Empire, he gathered together the leading authorities of Christianity for what is known as the Council of Nicaea so they could all hammer out their major theological differences. The end result was the official state religion of Rome.

So why is all this important? The church in Pergamum was commended for their faith, but they were then reproved for holding to the teaching of Balaam and the Nicolaitans. The Book of Numbers tells us that Balaam tried to prophesy a curse against Israel for the sake of money (see chapters 22 through 31). Balak, the king of Moab, was terrified of the prospect of the children of Israel coming into his land, so he hired Balaam to use his gift of prophecy against Israel. However, since God was on Israel's side, no matter what Balaam tried to do against Israel, it turned into a blessing instead. Balaam then tricked the Israelites into making an unholy alliance with the Moabites and eventually intermarrying with them. This was contrary to the will of God, and as a result the Israelites became polluted socially and spiritually. This is what is referred to in Revelation 2:14.

The second reproof the Lord gave was that some were also holding to the doctrine of the Nicolaitans. Remember that the church in Ephesus was commended for hating the works of the Nicolaitans, those who combined pagan practices with Christianity. A few centuries later the church was letting the teachings and doctrines of the Nicolaitans infiltrate their belief system. The Nicolaitans were trying to intermingle their occult practices with Christianity. That's like trying to mix oil with water—they just don't mix!

Why are these things important to note? While Constantine may have truly converted to Christianity, he certainly got things mixed up quite badly. What was created by the Council of Nicaea was Catholicism, not Christianity. Some might say that Catholicism and Christianity are the same thing, but they are far from it. As Catholicism developed, things such as idol worship and offering gifts to idols were incorporated into the religion. The idols were Mary, the apostles, and saints, and adherents to Catholicism bowed down to them, offered flowers, and lit candles in worship of these idols.

So the reproof of the church of Pergamum was justified. Pure and true Christianity was being transmuted into Catholicism, and this was something the Lord reproved and condemned. The Lord's counsel to the church of Pergamum was to repent, to turn away from the teachings of Balaam and the Nicolaitans. He also warned them that failure to repent would cause Him to war against them with the sword that comes out of His mouth. This should scare anyone! Hebrews 10:31 states, "It is a fearful thing to fall into the hands of the living God." I would not want God to come against me for any reason! But this is what the Christians during the church age of Pergamum would face if they did not repent.

The Lord said He would use the sword of His mouth against those who did not repent. The sword of His mouth is His Word, the Bible. We know this from Ephesians 6:17, which refers to "the sword of the Spirit, which is the word of God." There is great wisdom in this. When we are faced with teachings that are contrary to the Word of God, just as the church of Pergamum was faced with the teachings of Balaam and the Nicolaitans, we need to use the Word of God to combat the lies with the truth and to expose doctrinal mistakes and false teachings.

The church of Pergamum was left with a word of encouragement—those who overcome would be given a white stone with a new name known only to the Lord and the one to whom the stone was given. Imagine receiving such a gift from God—a white stone with a new name He personally chose for you that only you two would ever know. That is a personal relationship so deep and profound that I can't even begin to imagine how it would feel. It is the kind of relationship the Lord wants to have with you.

THE CHURCH OF THYATIRA (AD 600–AD 1517)

We find the Lord Jesus's message to the church in Thyatira in Revelation 2:18–27:

> To the angel of the church in Thyatira write:
> The Son of God, who has eyes like a flame of fire, and whose feet are like fine brass, says these things: I know your works, love, service, faith, and your patience, and that your last works are more than the first.
> But I have a few things against you: You permit that woman Jezebel, who calls herself a prophetess, to teach and seduce My servants to commit sexual immorality and eat food sacrificed to idols. I gave her time to repent of her sexual immorality, but she did not repent. Look! I will throw her onto a sickbed, and those who commit adultery with her into great tribulation, unless they repent of their deeds. I will put her children to death, and all the churches shall know that I am He who searches the hearts and minds. I will give to each one of you according to your deeds.
> Now to you I say, and to the rest in Thyatira, as many as do not have this teaching, who have not known what some call the "depths of Satan," I will put on you no other burden. But hold firmly what you have until I come.
> To him who overcomes and keeps My works to the end, I will give authority over the nations—He

"shall rule them with a rod of iron; like the vessels of
a potter they shall be broken in pieces"—even as I
myself have received authority from My Father.

Let's once again examine the four elements found in the
description of this particular church age.

- **Commendation**—"I know your works, love,
  service, faith, and your patience, and that
  your last works are more than the first."

- **Reproof**—"You permit that woman Jezebel,
  who calls herself a prophetess, to teach and
  seduce My servants to commit sexual immorality and eat food sacrificed to idols."

- **Counsel**—"Hold firmly what you have until
  I come."

- **Encouragement**—"To him who overcomes
  and keeps My works to the end, I will give
  authority over the nations—He 'shall rule
  them with a rod of iron; like the vessels of
  a potter they shall be broken in pieces'—
  even as I myself have received authority
  from My Father. And I will give him the
  morning star."

The church age of Thyatira covers the time period known
as the Dark Ages. Even in the midst of the Dark Ages the
church was doing things that pleased the Lord—they did
good works, they were loving, they served the Lord, they
had faith, and they were patient. The Lord commended

them for their works. I hate to admit this, but in my day and age such things are no longer easily found.

In Christ's reproof of Thyatira He spoke of a woman named Jezebel. Jezebel is a symbol of Catholicism, the religion that was seducing true born-again Christians to leave their faith behind and join her. Many true believers adhered to Catholicism because of its power and because they feared dying. Remember, you could be killed for denying or speaking out against Catholicism back then.

When born-again Christians left Christianity to join Catholicism, they committed spiritual fornication; they left Jesus Christ for something else. And just as bad, Christ pointed out that this spiritual Jezebel, this harlot, also caused many of the children of God to fall for her teachings and to eat food that had been offered up to idols. Many Christians failed the test. Instead of enduring all the trials and tribulations of the Dark Ages, including religious persecution, many caved in and became Catholics. This was a very dark time for the true Christian faith.

As dark as things were for the church, our Lord and Savior Jesus Christ counseled them to hold firmly to what they had until He came. This counsel is sage advice for those who are now living during the Tribulation. Revelation 17 warned that this same Jezebel spirit, the harlot, would set up her false religion (an occult one) for everyone on the earth to follow during the Tribulation. So if you became a born-again Christian after reading chapter 10, then just like the church of Thyatira you need to hold fast to your faith until Jesus returns. If you haven't become a born-again Christian yet, allow me to encourage you to do it now. You are living during the Tribulation, and at any moment you may be killed or imprisoned for even the smallest of infractions. Secure your eternal life in heaven now while you still can.

Christ's encouragement to the church of Thyatira was once again directed to those who overcome. To paraphrase it, Christ said He will give them a leadership position and authority in His new kingdom, and He will give them the morning star (meaning He will give of Himself to His children, the star being a symbol of the glory of God).[4] Many Christians in my day and age are going to receive heavenly gifts from Jesus Christ for what they did for His service while they were alive. To teach; to preach; to do good deeds; to help the poor and the widows; to visit those in prison; to lead people to salvation; and if necessary, to die a martyr's death—these are some of the things our Lord wants us to do. This will remain true even in your time. Christ encourages us to do these things because they are part of what we have become because of Him. We become compassionate, we become caring, and we become loving. So keep His works to the end. Your reward will be great.

You are living during the most dangerous period in human history. Depending on how far you are into the Tribulation, the Antichrist has either already risen or will soon rise to power and become the global dictator. Think carefully about what you're going to do next. Follow the Antichrist or follow Jesus Christ—your eternity rests upon your decision.

The church of Thyatira was the last church age addressed in Revelation 2. In the next chapter we will turn our attention to the last three church ages, which are addressed in Revelation 3.

Chapter 12
THE FINAL AGES OF THE CHURCH

W<small>E WILL NOW</small> turn our attention to the final three ages of the church: Sardis, Philadelphia, and Laodicea. We will examine the historical background of each age and delve into what Jesus Christ had to say to each of the churches. Let's get started.

THE CHURCH OF SARDIS
(AD 1517–AD 1750)

Jesus's message to the church of Sardis, representing the fifth church age, is found in Revelation 3:1–6:

> To the angel of the church in Sardis write:
>
> He who has the seven Spirits of God and the seven stars says these things: I know your works, that you have a reputation of being alive, but you are dead. Be watchful, and strengthen the things which remain but are ready to die, for I have not found your works perfected before God. Remember therefore how you have received and heard; hold fast and repent. Therefore if you will not watch, I will come upon you as a thief, and you will not know what hour I will come upon you.
>
> You have a few names even in Sardis who have not soiled their garments. They shall walk with Me in white, for they are worthy. He who overcomes shall be clothed in white garments. I will not blot

his name out of the Book of Life, but I will confess
his name before My Father and before His angels.
He who has an ear, let him hear what the Spirit says
to the churches.

As with all the others, we find four elements in the
description of this church age.

- **Commendation**—"You have a few names
  even in Sardis who have not soiled their
  garments."

- **Reproof**—"You are dead....I have not found
  your works perfected before God."

- **Counsel**—"Be watchful, and strengthen
  the things which remain but are ready to
  die....Remember therefore how you have
  received and heard; hold fast and repent."

- **Encouragement**—"They shall walk with Me
  in white, for they are worthy. He who over-
  comes shall be clothed in white garments.
  I will not blot his name out of the Book of
  Life, but I will confess his name before My
  Father and before His angels."

The church age associated with the church of Sardis
began in 1517 with the start of the Protestant Reformation.
During the last three hundred years or so of the previous
church age, there were a few born-again Christians and
certain others who stood up to the Catholic Church and
said, "Enough is enough!" Those who stood up and spoke
out against the false teachings and doctrines of the Catholic

Church were eventually called "Protestants" because they protested against the Catholic Church. Men such as Jan Hus, Peter Waldo, and John Wycliffe attempted to reveal the unscriptural practices, teachings, and doctrines of the Catholic Church, but nothing really seemed to make a lasting impact until 1517.

On October 31, 1517, priest and scholar Martin Luther nailed a copy of his Ninety-Five Theses to the door of the church in Wittenberg, Germany. The document spelled out many major flaws in the Catholic religion. Needless to say, this produced a lot of trouble because Luther was, after all, a Catholic priest. The Ninety-Five Theses were reprinted and widely distributed, sparking the Reformation. When Luther refused to recant his views, Pope Leo X formally excommunicated him. However, despite the excommunication, Luther's work formed the basis of the Protestant Reformation, which dramatically affected Western civilization.

I am convinced that a number of born-again Christians who turned away from the original teachings of Christ in order to become Catholics changed their minds and went back to true Christianity as born-again Christians because of the Reformation. The movement provided them with a voice, and they were able to stand up with their fellow believers and say no to the false teachings of Catholicism.

In His reproof of the church of Sardis, Christ said that He knew their works and that they had a reputation of being alive. We can glean from this that some born-again Christians were still being faithful to Christ and doing what Christians should be striving to do. This is confirmed in Christ's admonishment to "strengthen the things which remain." There was at least a little of what was right and true left within the church.

However, the Lord's reproof indicates that despite the church's reputation of being alive, they were dead. This implies that as a whole, the vast majority of born-again Christians during this church age were spiritually dead. The question is, why? What caused the church that had previously been an unstoppable, burning flame for the Lord to become spiritually dead? Let me explain.

The Lord's counsel to the church of Sardis was to be watchful, strengthen the things that remained but were ready to die, remember how they received and heard, hold fast, and repent. This counsel includes five things for us to learn and do.

Be watchful

To be watchful is to be aware of what is occurring or being said so you can quickly discern when something does not line up with the Word of God, the Bible. During this church age the Reformation occurred. Yet there were two very serious deficiencies. The church lacked proper instruction in Bible prophecy, and they did not separate themselves from the mainline religion, Catholicism. True born-again Christians who are watchful are more prone to be separated from any mainline religion and hold fast to the prophecies, especially those of the imminent return of Jesus Christ during the rapture.

Strengthen the things that remain but are ready to die

This refers to the sound doctrinal teachings of the early days of the Reformation, which taught salvation by faith, the total depravity of man, and the Bible being the authoritative Word of God. These are the things that need to be strengthened and held to with tenacity.

Remember how you received and heard

People received and heard the truth of the gospel through searching the Bible and reading God's Word for themselves and through reliable preaching based on the Word of God. The truth comes by hearing the Word of God, not through man-made religion or false rituals.

Hold fast

This is a very clear warning to tenaciously cling to the Word of God and sound Bible teaching. The Word of God is powerful, and we need to hold on to it with all our might.

Repent

Repentance is turning away from sin and turning to God. It also involves a submissive heart, one that wants to do the will of God.

The message to the church of Sardis also indicated that there were some who had not soiled their garments. They were the born-again Christians who held to the Word of God and followed it to the best of their abilities. They did not follow the false teachings and doctrines. They steadfastly clung to the teachings of Jesus Christ no matter what the cost, and many were martyred during this time period because they refused to follow false teachings.

Christ's encouragement for those who did not soil their garments and who overcame was that they would be clothed in white garments and walk with Him. I can't even begin to imagine what a phenomenal honor that must be—to be able to walk by the Lord's side is something I just can't wrap my mind around. We are speaking of God, Jesus Christ, the Lord, the Creator of everything. Words just fail me.

Christ also told us He would not blot out their names from the Book of Life. Those who are saved will not have their names removed but will be with God for eternity. However, those who are not saved and do not have their names written in the Book of Life will be cast into the lake of fire for eternity (Rev. 20:15). So if you haven't already become a born-again Christian, please consider doing it now. You know as well as I do that time is running out.

THE CHURCH OF PHILADELPHIA (AD 1750–AD 1920)

We learn of the church age of Philadelphia in Revelation 3:7–13:

> To the angel of the church in Philadelphia write:
> He who is holy, He who is true, He who has the key of David, He who opens and no one shuts, and shuts and no one opens, says these things: I know your works. Look! I have set before you an open door, and no one can shut it. For you have a little strength, and have kept My word, and have not denied My name. Listen! I will make them of the synagogue of Satan, who say they are Jews and are not, but lie. Listen! I will make them come and worship before your feet and to know that I have loved you. Because you have kept My word of patience, I also will keep you from the hour of temptation which shall come upon the entire world, to test those who dwell on the earth.
> Look, I am coming quickly. Hold firmly what

you have, so that no one may take your crown. He who overcomes will I make a pillar in the temple of My God, and he shall go out no more. I will write on him the name of My God and the name of the city of My God, the New Jerusalem, which comes down out of heaven from My God, and My own new name. He who has an ear, let him hear what the Spirit says to the churches.

Before examining the historical background of this church age, let's see what Christ had to say about the church of Philadelphia.

- **Commendation**—"You have a little strength, and have kept My word, and have not denied My name."

- **Reproof**—There is not one word of correction.

- **Counsel**—"Hold firmly what you have, so that no one may take your crown."

- **Encouragement**—"He who overcomes will I make a pillar in the temple of My God, and he shall go out no more. I will write on him the name of My God and the name of the city of My God, the New Jerusalem, which comes down out of heaven from My God, and My own new name."

During the last church age we examined, Sardis, our brothers and sisters in Christ were struggling to hold on to the teachings of God's Word. They were standing up against the false teachings of Catholicism, and even in the face of death many of them did not budge. They held firm to their faith in Jesus Christ. This went on for more than two centuries until the church age of Philadelphia arrived. The word *Philadelphia* means "brotherly love." The spirit of Philadelphia spread throughout Europe and America.

The spirit of Philadelphia was the great revival movement that began during this time period. The Dark Ages were long over, and the Spanish Inquisition was beginning to lose its grip over Europe and other countries. Movable type print had been created, so everyone could get a copy of the Holy Bible written in the common man's language. Revival was happening throughout the world. Born-again Christians were on fire for the Lord, and the teachings of salvation were sweeping the land. These events led to the greatest missionary and evangelical movement in Christian history.

One of the great evangelists of this time period was named Billy Sunday. Billy Sunday was born in 1862. He began a career as a professional baseball player in the 1880s. In 1886 Billy was out on the town in Chicago with his teammates. He happened upon some street preaching, and he became a born-again Christian because of the outreach of Pacific Garden Mission. After he became a Christian, Billy's teammates and fans began to notice a difference in him. He gave up alcohol and started speaking at various churches and YMCAs.[1] In 1891 Billy rejected a lucrative baseball contract and accepted a position with the Chicago YMCA. His new position entailed a lot of ministerial work, preparing him for his future as an evangelist.[2]

In 1893 Billy became the full-time assistant to well-known evangelist J. Wilbur Chapman. Billy Sunday acted as Chapman's "advance man," and he organized prayer meetings, music, venues, and all the other details in the cities where Chapman would be preaching. Chapman mentored Billy and helped him develop as a preacher and evangelist while encouraging him to place a strong emphasis on prayer.[3]

During his lifetime Billy Sunday preached to an estimated one hundred million people, and it is estimated that over a million people became born-again Christians as a result of Billy's preaching. He estimated that he preached around twenty thousand sermons. He died one week after preaching his last sermon, the text of which was, "What must I do to be saved?"[4]

The church age of Philadelphia produced some of the greatest preachers and evangelists in Christian history. Revival hit many countries, people were convicted of their sins and saved, and the name of Christ was exalted above all others. And one person, one born-again Christian, can make a difference. Look at what Billy Sunday accomplished by surrendering his life to Jesus Christ. Think of the difference you could make as a born-again Christian. It only takes one person to start a movement.

Christ told us that the church of Philadelphia had a little strength, had kept His Word, and had not denied His name. Revival broke out during this church age because people were following the Word of God and they didn't deny God by hiding their belief or faith in Him. As a result, people were getting saved everywhere. As impossible as this may sound to you in the future, such a thing is still possible if enough people become saved, follow God's Word, and do not deny Him, whatever the cost. Let me encourage you by saying this: millions of people can become saved during your day and age, when the world has been handed over to the Antichrist. You will hear of people denying the Antichrist and his so-called power and instead turning to Jesus Christ. You need to get saved now and band together with those who are also following Jesus Christ. Your strength will not only lie in numbers but also in keeping God's Word, not denying Christ, and believing in the cause of righteousness. You must stand up in faith and boldly show that even though the world has been plunged into darkness, the light of Christ is still out there to be seen.

When I reflect on the church of Philadelphia, what I find most remarkable is that Christ did not need to reprove them for anything. Our brothers and sisters in Christ were doing everything right for the Lord. Now that doesn't mean they weren't sinners. They still had their flaws, but they didn't let their flaws or sins get in their way of witnessing for Jesus Christ and leading others to salvation.

The advice or counsel the Lord gave to the church of Philadelphia was to hold firmly to what they had so that no one could take their crown. Rewards will be given to God's children when they enter heaven, including different crowns to the children of God who merit them. Christ was telling the church of Philadelphia to keep doing what they were doing—don't let go, and don't stop. From my personal perspective, let me add this: don't worry about your rewards in heaven. Do good things because it's the right thing to do. That will be extremely difficult at times, because you are living during the Tribulation. Christians in the past faced many of the same horrible conditions you're going through, and many died as martyrs because they would not deny their faith in Jesus Christ. They held firmly to Jesus and His Word, and so should you.

The church of Philadelphia was encouraged with three things. First, Jesus said those who overcame would be pillars in the temple of God. Pillars represent stability, and for a Christian they represent faith in Jesus Christ—it is the stability needed during tough times and temptations or when facing rejection or martyrdom for faith in Jesus Christ. There will be a special position for those who place their complete faith and trust in the Lord.

Christ's second word of encouragement states that He will write the name of God and the name of the city of God on them. This name indicates that the person bearing it is a follower of Jesus Christ and is allowed entrance into the city of God.

The third word of encouragement says that Christ will write upon them His new name. This very special blessing denotes that the person bearing the name of Christ belongs to Jesus Christ Himself. That person is one of God's children and is forever under His divine glory in heaven. What a future that is to look forward to.

THE CHURCH OF LAODICEA (AD 1920–RAPTURE)

The church age associated with the church of Laodicea is the time period I am living in right now as I write this book. It is the final church age in Christian history and is described in Revelation 3:14–22:

> To the angel of the church of the Laodiceans write:
> The Amen, the Faithful and True Witness, the Beginning of the creation of God, says these things:

I know your works, that you are neither cold nor hot. I wish you were cold or hot. So then, because you are lukewarm, and neither cold nor hot, I will spit you out of My mouth. For you say, "I am rich, and have stored up goods, and have need of nothing," yet do not realize that you are wretched, miserable, poor, blind, and naked. I counsel you to buy from Me gold refined by fire, that you may be rich, and white garments, that you may be dressed, that the shame of your nakedness may not appear, and anoint your eyes with eye salve, that you may see.

Those whom I love, I rebuke and discipline. Therefore be zealous and repent. Listen! I stand at the door and knock. If anyone hears My voice and opens the door, I will come in and dine with him, and he with Me.

To him who overcomes will I grant to sit with Me on My throne, as I also overcame and sat down with My Father on His throne. He who has an ear, let him hear what the Spirit says to the churches.

Let's take a look at the four elements found in the description of the final church age, the age of Laodicea.

- **Commendation**—There is not one word of commendation in this passage.

- **Reproof**—"You are neither cold nor hot.…For you say, 'I am rich, and have stored up goods, and have need of nothing,' yet do not realize that you are wretched, miserable, poor, blind, and naked."

- **Counsel**—"I counsel you to buy from Me gold refined by fire, that you may be

rich, and white garments, that you may be
dressed, that the shame of your nakedness
may not appear, and anoint your eyes with
eye salve, that you may see…be zealous
and repent."

- **Encouragement**—"To him who overcomes
will I grant to sit with Me on My throne."

During the Laodicean church age, the majority of our
brothers and sisters in Christ became lukewarm—they
were neither hot nor cold. They were fence walkers, people
who walk down the middle and won't commit one way
or the other. Christ was telling us that Christians lost the
fire and passion they had for Him during the Philadelphia
church age and ended up as nothing more than lukewarm.

Have you ever been outside playing some sort of rig-
orous sport and gone to the kitchen faucet to get a glass
of water? Have you ever suddenly realized as you were
drinking that the water was lukewarm and not the cold,
refreshing drink you wanted? I know I have. Once that
lukewarm water hit my mouth, I spit it out in the sink and
emptied out the glass. It left a very unpleasant feeling in my
mouth, and it certainly wasn't what I was looking for. This
is how Christ is looking at His children during the final
church. We are spiritually lukewarm, and because we are
only lukewarm, Christ can't use us. Christ symbolically
spits us out of His mouth, saying, "You are no good to Me."
Again, it's like being a fence walker—because we haven't
committed one way or the other, Christ can't use us. We
have become the worst examples of what Christianity is
supposed to represent. It's because of this that Christ gave
us no commendation.

Our spiritual condition in the church age of Laodicea is so bad and pathetic that Christ used the following adjectives to describe our spiritual state of existence:

- Wretched

- Miserable

- Poor

- Blind

- Naked

Every single one of these adjectives speaks out against our spiritual state of existence. We are wretched people, people who are unhappy. Many Christians living during this church age are spiritually unhappy because they are not being fed the Word of God from the pulpit. But quite honestly, most of them don't want to be the truth of God's Word. They want to go to church, get their Sunday morning fix, and then live like the devil for the rest of the week. That is not Christianity—that's living in the world and becoming part of the problems that infest this world like a spiritual cancer slowly eating away at their spirits until they become spiritually dead. They end up as miserable Christians because they did what the world told them to do instead of living according to God's instructions.

Laodicean Christians are also spiritually poor. If they were a grocery store, their shelves would be empty. They are so spiritually bankrupt that they are like beggars looking for crumbs to eat. Instead of eating from the Word of God, they eat what the world feeds them. But the world's food kills us spiritually. Let's play another game on our game consoles, mindlessly text everyone we know, surf the Internet, and spend countless hours on social media. Let's do anything but read the Word of God and get some real meat into our spiritual bellies so we can spiritually learn and grow.

Christ also said we are blind. The reason for this spiritual blindness is blatantly obvious—we are not reading the Word of God. We lost the ability to teach ourselves. We are spoiled by modern conveniences and spend our time entertaining ourselves instead of learning from God's most holy and precious Word.

The Laodicean church is also deceived. They think they have need of nothing, when in fact the opposite is true (Rev. 3:17). I would even say they are living in a state of self-deception. Galatians 6:3 says, "For if someone thinks himself to be something when he is nothing, he deceives himself." The Laodicean church is characterized by people who think going to church on Sunday is all that is needed. Their lives are characterized by a desire for comfort and entertainment rather than a hunger and thirst for righteousness and the truth of God's Word. They don't grow spiritually or take advantage of the incredible gift of communicating with the Creator of the universe through prayer.

Laodicean Christians are spiritually sick individuals. They are wretched, miserable, poor, blind, and naked (Rev. 3:17). The most startling thing about all of this is that they don't have to be that way. No one has to exist in such a poor spiritual state. You can always stand up, brush yourself off, and move forward with the Lord. You don't have to live in a spiritually bankrupt state. The Lord instructed the Laodicean church about how to be spiritually healed:

Buy from Me gold refined by fire

In other words, purify yourself spiritually so that you can be used and blessed by God. Allow the riches of the Word of God to refine you and take away all your impurities. The Word of God tells us that the Lord is "like a refiner's fire" (Mal. 3:2). The Word also says God "will refine them as the refinement of silver, and will test them as the testing of gold. They will call on My name, and I will answer them. I will say, 'They are My people'; and they will say, 'The LORD is my God'" (Zech. 13:9).

Buy from Me...white garments

The white garments are another symbol of purity. These garments from God cover spiritual nakedness. People who proclaim Christianity and don't live it are quickly discovered and their spiritual nakedness becomes very evident. The Book of Romans tells us to put on Christ (the way you would put on a garment):

> Furthermore, knowing the time, now is the moment to awake from sleep. For now our salvation is nearer than when we believed. The night is far spent, the day is at hand. Therefore let us take off the works of darkness and put on the armor of light. Let us behave properly, as in the day, not in carousing and drunkenness, not in immorality and wickedness, not in strife and envy. But put on the Lord Jesus Christ, and make no provision for the flesh to fulfill its lusts.
>
> —ROMANS 13:11–14

So put on Christ like a garment and do not make provision for sin in your life.

Anoint your eyes with eye salve

Imagine you were physically blind. You would have to use a number of alternative methods to accomplish certain tasks. For example, when pouring a cup of coffee, you might hold the tip of your thumb against the inside of the cup, allowing you to determine how much coffee to pour into the cup. Once the coffee reached the desired level, you would feel the heat of the coffee with the tip of your thumb. It is a clever trick that would work well. As Christians in the age of Laodicea, most of us tried various "tricks" to live our lives as so-called Christians. We may have fooled others, but we certainly did not fool Jesus Christ. He reproved us for our blindness. But He also offered us a solution. He said to anoint our eyes with eye salve so that we could see again.

In medicine, salves or medical pastes are used on serious cuts and bruises and such. There are also certain salves to put around the eye if it is infected. The eye salve Christ spoke of was a spiritual eye salve that would restore the person's eyesight. That eye salve is the Word of God, the Holy Bible. If born-again Christians would read their Bibles like they used to, they would no longer be spiritually blind. They would be able to see this world and its corruption as they really are. They would stop being lukewarm, give up doing things their way, and once again begin doing things God's way. However, in my day and age, the age of Laodicea, I see more spiritually blind Christians than those with spiritual vision. Yet at this point in my life, even though I am living during the Laodicean church age, I have also seen many Christian brothers and sisters starting to see again. At some of the conventions and conferences I have attended or spoken at, you could almost physically feel how spiritually hungry some of the attendees were. I have seen Christians being spiritually fed and coming alive with the knowledge they were receiving. You could see it in their eyes and on their faces. It gave me hope for the Laodicean church.

One thing I want you to be aware of is that due to the day and age you're living in, you are going to be tempted very quickly to surrender your Christian values to the forces of darkness and the Antichrist. You need to stand your ground no matter what may happen. Many horrible things are going to happen, but you must be better at Christianity than the Laodicean Christians were. You will be used as a beacon of light to help others get saved during the Tribulation. God will be able to work miracles through you if you allow Him to.

The only saving grace for the church of Laodicea is found in the Lord's encouragement to me and every one of my Christian brothers and sisters who are living now: those who overcome will sit with Jesus on His throne just as Jesus overcame and sat with His Father on the throne. When God took on His physical form and was known as Jesus Christ, He lived a human life just like you and me. He overcame this world by not becoming a part of it. He didn't sin. He lived according to His Word, the Bible. This may be a difficult concept for you to grasp at first, but in His physical form Jesus Christ was just as human as you and I and was subjected to temptation to make Him sin. I know that's a tricky one to wrap your mind around, but look at it this way—it would take God to do it. And He did! Satan tried every possible way to get Jesus Christ to stumble and sin, but Jesus did not succumb to Satan or the tricks and snares of this world. Jesus was victorious in all ways, and because He overcame the world, He sits on a throne in heaven. And this is what He is offering everyone who is a born-again Christian during the Laodicean church age. If we overcome all of the self-deception and temptations that prevent us from being used by God and show the world what it means to be a true born-again Christian, then He will also allow us to sit with Him on His throne. So despite the flaws, faults, and sins during this day and age, there is still hope left for us. It is up to my brothers and sisters in Christ right now to decide whether we will be on fire for Christ again or like a match that was blown out by the wind. I can only pray that my brothers and sisters will once again stand up before it's too late and make a difference for the name of Jesus Christ and for His kingdom.

There is one more thing I want to point out before we end our discussion of the church age of Laodicea. Earlier in the book I stated there were three entities responsible for you ending up in the Tribulation. One of them was you. You have responsibility for your own choices, and you were not saved (a born-again Christian) when the rapture hit, so you remained on the earth to face the Tribulation. (But, Lord willing, you will get saved before it's over with, if you have not gotten saved already.) The second one to blame is Satan. Through his demons you were deceived into not becoming a born-again Christian at one time or another in your life before the rapture happened. For whatever reason, you chose not to get saved when you had the opportunity.

The third one responsible for your present predicament is me—well, me and other born-again Christians who lived during the church age of Laodicea. We had the numbers; there were plenty of Christians who could have gone out and witnessed. But we didn't. We no longer had that zeal, that drive to save the lost, and that is most assuredly part of the reason you are living during the Tribulation. I am so very sorry we failed you. We let you down. We preferred to be entertained than to do the work of God. Please forgive us.

Yet you are not without hope. It is for this reason that this book has been written—so that you could have hope. Remember that God has not abandoned you. He is still trying to get your attention so you can get saved and eventually be with Him in heaven along with the rest of us. He loves you. He cares for you. He is still trying to reach out to you. Remember this always. And remember that if you haven't chosen to get saved yet, you can get saved at any time while you are still alive. But be warned: the Tribulation will last only seven years, and many people will die during its catastrophic events. You don't have forever to choose between God and Satan. If you don't get saved, you automatically reject God and by default choose Satan. Whatever decision you make will be an eternal one that can never be changed.

The age of Christianity has come and gone. The seven church ages ended when Christ appeared in the clouds and all born-again Christians were called up to meet Him. But what about now? For those of you living during the Tribulation, what happens next? What can you expect as the events of the Tribulation unfold? Once again we will turn to the Holy Bible for the answers.

Chapter 13
THE SEVEN SEALS

T HE BOOK OF Revelation tells us that John saw an open door in heaven. He heard a voice with the strength and volume of a trumpet that said, "Come up here, and I will show you things which must take place after this" (Rev. 4:1).

If you remember, the apostle John was given the responsibility to write the Book of Revelation, which served as the Lord's warning of the things that would happen during the seven church ages and beyond that into the Tribulation period. That is the same thing I'm trying to do for you with this book. I am trying to warn you of the things you can expect to happen during the Tribulation and, Lord willing, help you through them the best way I can with my understanding of the events described in the Bible.

After the apostle John heard the voice of God say, "Come up here," he was immediately taken up to heaven in the Spirit. Revelation 4 and 5 give us a glimpse of what transpired in heaven, within the very realm of God Himself. However, our interest is more with the things that are taking place and will be taking place during the Tribulation. I suggest reading about the heavenly events later in a Bible that I pray you will be able to find. The one detail you do need to know from those chapters is that there is a scroll with seven seals (Rev. 5:1).

Keep in mind that the Book of Revelation is full of symbols, more so than any other book in the Bible. It is for this reason alone that many born-again Christians during my time never read it, saying it was too hard to understand. That was just another symptom of lukewarm Christianity. The truth of the matter is that God would not have given us the Book of Revelation or any other book of the Bible if they were too hard to understand. Granted, you do have to put some effort into understanding all the symbolism; but the Book of Revelation gives us our best understanding of what you are living through right now. Don't worry about all of the symbolism or the details. I am writing this book as a Christian brother and teacher to guide you and help you understand the things happening in your day and age. Having said all that, let's take a look at what happens as the seven seals are opened.

THE FIRST SEAL

In Revelation 6:1 the first seal is opened, or broken. Once that occurs, a white horse appears on the scene with a rider upon it. The rider has a bow in one hand and a crown on his head (Rev. 6:2). This bowman is the Antichrist, the ultimate enemy of Christ and all of His followers (born-again Christians). He is let loose on the earth to conquer it; however, he doesn't do it at first. Notice that the Antichrist has a bow but there is no arrow in it. When the Antichrist first appears, he will do so as a man of peace. After all, he is trying to get the world to follow him, so he does not want to show up as a roaring lion. But later on his true nature shall be revealed.

If you're living during the very early days of the Tribulation, a man who appears to be a man of peace is going to come on the scene and begin to unite the world. The swiftest way to accomplish this would be if the Antichrist was a politician in a country that has a sudden, overnight, meteoric rise. He will be a very persuasive guy and appear to be a man of peace on the surface. If you haven't seen or heard of such a person yet, watch out for him in the newspapers or on the television.

THE SECOND SEAL

Next, the second seal is broken and another horse appears. This horse is red and has a rider with the power to take peace away from the world and cause people to kill each other. The rider upon the red horse is carrying a "great sword" (Rev. 6:3–4). This sword symbolically represents the wars that the second rider will bring upon the earth. The red color of the horse represents all the death and the blood that will be spilled because of the red rider. This will work in the favor of the Antichrist, because he is supposed to bring the entire world into a state of peace.

THE THIRD SEAL

The third seal is broken next, and a black horse with a rider shows up on the scene. The rider is holding a pair of scales in his hand. What is the purpose of the scales? A voice in heaven proclaims, "A quart of wheat for a day's wages, and three quarts of barley for a day's wages" (Rev. 6:5–6).

Let's take a look at what is going to be measured on the scales of the black rider. We are told that a quart of wheat will cost a day's wages and three measures of barley (a much lesser grain) will also cost a day's wages. It takes around a quart of wheat to make a loaf of bread. Therefore, three quarts of barley would make around three loaves of barley bread. In other words, in your day and age you will have to do a full day's worth of labor just to have enough money to buy a loaf of bread. This will be due to a global food shortage. Because of hyperinflation, it will be very expensive to buy even a loaf of bread. In my time a loaf of bread costs on average around $2.40.[1] Minimum wage in the United States right now is $7.25. If a loaf of bread cost me a day's wages, it would cost $58. And that is based on minimum wage!

After World War I, Germany experienced hyperinflation. In September 1923 a loaf of bread, which cost half a mark in 1918, cost 1.5 *million* marks.[2] In your day it may be even worse. Money will be all but worthless, and food will be scarce. Any sort of government aid will be gone. How will anyone be able to feed their family if they're only making enough money to feed themselves? This will be just the beginning of the end for those living in the Tribulation period.

THE FOURTH SEAL

When the fourth seal is broken, we immediately see a pale horse and a rider on the earth. This horse is a greenish, sickly looking color. The rider on this horse is Death, and Hell or Hades is following right behind him. Hell is following immediately behind Death because a fourth of the entire world's population will be killed by war, starvation, and wild beasts that will hunt down mankind as food because there will be almost nothing left for the animals to eat either (Rev. 6:7–8).

As I write this portion of this book, the population of the earth is just over seven and a half billion people. Since

I am writing this section of the book to reach you in the future, let's say that in your day and age the population of the earth has reached eight billion. That means two billion people will die as a result of war, hunger, and wild animals. The earth's population will quickly drop from eight billion people to six billion people. If you live through this part of the Tribulation, you will be witnessing so much death and carnage that people won't even be able to bury all the dead. There will be piles of bodies around the world as people desperately try to find a place to bury two billion corpses that will swiftly start to rot.

We are also instructed that Hell is following right behind Death. The sad reason this is true is because the majority of people still are not saved, and because they did not accept Jesus Christ and get saved, upon their death they immediately end up in hell. Think about this very carefully if you are not saved yet.

THE FIFTH SEAL

When the fifth seal is opened, we find that "the souls of those who had been slain for the word of God and for the testimony they had held" are underneath the altar in heaven (Rev. 6:9). These are the souls of all those in your day and age who became born-again Christians and would not renounce Jesus Christ and His Word.

As I explained before, even during the Tribulation, while the inhabitants of Earth are being punished for their sins, God is still trying to reach out to them and get their attention by telling them to get saved before it's too late. But the vast majority of those who do get saved will be killed because they will not follow the Antichrist or any of his deceptions. Those Christians will stand up and oppose

159

the Antichrist with their voices and with the Word of God on their lips. They will surely die as martyrs because, among other things, they will try to reach out to you and everyone else about salvation and Jesus Christ, warning that you must get saved before it's too late.

The Sixth Seal

When the sixth seal is broken, catastrophes in many forms will happen. Here is a list of what you will personally witness (assuming you survived the opening of the fourth seal):

A great earthquake will happen

The sun will turn black

The moon will turn red

The stars of heaven will fall to the earth

The heavens will roll back as a papyrus scroll

Every mountain and island will be moved out of its place (Rev. 6:12–14)

So when you least expect it, a great earthquake will happen. Notice that the Bible teaches us that this will be no ordinary earthquake. It is emphasized to be a "great" earthquake. This could very well be a magnitude 10 earthquake that scientists in my day admitted was a possibility.[3] As of the writing of this book, it is commonly believed that the San Andreas Fault in California is overdue for an earthquake.[4] That fault line is roughly eight hundred miles long, and a significant earthquake along even a portion of the fault line would be catastrophic. If the great earthquake that occurs during the Tribulation is not the San Andreas Fault finally giving in, then it will be another great earthquake somewhere around the world. Hundreds of thousands, perhaps even millions of people may die because of this one event.

We next find out that the sun will turn black, the moon will turn red, the stars of heaven will fall to the earth, the heavens will roll back as a scroll, and every mountain and island will be moved out of its normal position. There are a number of events that could possibly cause all five of these events to happen.

In the Pacific Ocean is an area known as the Ring of Fire. This area forms a 25,000-mile ring in the shape of a horseshoe. It contains 452 volcanoes, including 75 percent of the world's active volcanoes.[5] Over 80 percent of the largest earthquakes happen there.[6] What causes me even greater fear for those living during the Tribulation is the fact that within the Ring of Fire there are also supervolcanoes. A supervolcanic eruption could affect the entire planet. If a supervolcano had a major eruption of magnitude 8, it would fill the atmosphere with ash, sulfuric acid, and sulfur dioxide, causing a volcanic winter and worldwide famine, potentially killing tens of millions of people.[7]

Photos have been taken of the moon and sun after a volcano eruption. Due to all the ash and soot thrown into the atmosphere, the moon suddenly appeared to turn red and the sun appeared to be black because the ash blotted it out.[8] And amazingly enough, a volcano can spew out clouds of tephra (pieces of magma that range in size from small particles of ash to house-sized boulders).[9] Large pieces of tephra may be similar in appearance to small comets or fire bombs. It could be that when the apostle John saw the stars of heaven falling, it was actually tephra. Remember, John was writing about things that would happen in the future and were often outside of his realm of knowledge.

John never saw a supervolcano erupt, so he would have a very difficult time describing such an event for us. Because the force of a supervolcano would be greater than thousands of atomic bombs going off,[10] the eruption could not only cause the clouds in the atmosphere to be forced away like a scroll, but it could also cause many islands and mountains to be moved out of their places. However, there could be another explanation for all of these events.

There are prophecies in the Bible that on the surface appear to be referring to nuclear detonations. In the Old Testament Zechariah 14:12 reads, "And this will be the pestilence with which the LORD will strike all the peoples who go to battle against Jerusalem: Their flesh will rot as they stand on their feet, their eyes will rot in their sockets, and their tongues will rot in their mouths." This is precisely what happened to the inhabitants of Hiroshima and Nagasaki when the first atomic bombs were used during World War II.[11]

In another book of the Bible, Ezekiel 38:22 reads, "And I will rain upon him and upon his troops and upon the many peoples who are with him, an overflowing rain and hailstones, fire and brimstone." This could very well be referring to nuclear bombs because the description fits the chain of events when a nuclear bomb is detonated. A possible pre-sign of a nuclear detonation occurring in your lifetime is the situation with Iran. For over a decade Iran has been producing plutonium, which is commonly used for nuclear bombs.[12] Even now President Trump is dealing with what the news is calling the "Iran Nuclear Crisis." A coincidence? I seriously doubt it, but I pray that's all it is because Iran has been hostile toward America for decades ever since Ayatollah Ruhollah Khomeini replaced the pro-American shah as a result of the 1979 revolution. Khomeini referred to the United States as the "Great Satan."[13] If nuclear bombs are the cause of every mountain and island moving out of place, then among the other horrors that mankind will have to face is radiation sickness. For those who live in close proximity to the sites of the detonations and have moderate to severe exposure to radiation, death could occur anywhere within a few days to a few weeks.[14] I pray that it's not nuclear weapons that will cause all of the events described in Revelation 6 to happen.

The only other reason that the sun would turn black, the moon would turn red, the stars of heaven would fall, the sky would roll back like a scroll, and every mountain and island would move out of its place is a supernatural reason—because of God. These events could simply be God using His creation to get the attention of everyone on the earth. Sometimes God uses extreme methods to get people's attention, and during the Tribulation I suppose He would have to use very drastic methods indeed. Revelation 6:15–17 tells us that when these events happen, people will try to hide in caves and among rocks because the events are so terrifying, saying to the mountains and rocks, "Fall on us, and hide us from the face of Him who sits on the throne, and from the wrath of the Lamb, for the great day of His wrath has come." In the midst of their terror people will realize that the day of God's wrath has come.

THE SEVENTH SEAL

When the seventh seal is broken, something very odd occurs. There is silence in heaven for half an hour (Rev. 8:1).

Whether or not this is a literal half hour by our measurement of time is uncertain. Nothing happens on the earth when the seventh seal is opened; there is only silence. But I believe this is the calm before the next storm breaks loose.

Let's review so we can begin to set up a timeline of events that will happen during the Tribulation. This will help you determine where on the timeline you are right now. You'll also be able to figure out what events haven't happened yet and prepare yourself for them.

- The first seal—A man of peace will arrive and seemingly solve all the problems of the world. He is identified in the Bible as the Antichrist.

- The second seal—Wars will suddenly break out, possibly around most of the world.

- The third seal—Currencies from around the world will become worthless due in part to hyperinflation. A global famine will occur, and a person will have to work a full day to make enough money to buy a loaf of bread.

- The fourth seal—One-fourth of the world's population (around two billion people) will be killed by war, famine, and wild animals. Many will end up in hell because they did not get saved when they had the chance.

- The fifth seal—People will end up as martyrs because they became born-again Christians. They will be killed, but they will go to heaven rather than hell.

- The sixth seal—A great earthquake will happen. The sun will turn black. The moon will turn red. The stars of heaven will fall. The heavens will be rolled back like a scroll. Every mountain and island will be moved out of its normal position.

- The seventh seal—Nothing will happen that has an immediate or physical effect upon you or the earth.

This is your timeline thus far. Multiple punishments will strike the earth as a result of the seven seals, but more will occur once we get into the seven trumpets in the next chapter. If you are beginning to see any of these events happening right now, then you are living during the very beginning of the Tribulation. If you've already seen or heard of all these events occurring, then you are past the beginning of the Tribulation. As we cover additional events described in the Book of Revelation, you will be able to determine where you are in the Tribulation timeline.

THE 144,000

We need to cover one more thing before we move on to the seven trumpets. Revelation 7:1–8 says that twelve thousand people from each of the twelve tribes of Israel will be chosen by God for a very special mission. The 144,000 of Israel will be sealed with the seal of the living God on their foreheads.

Without trying to get into all of the nitty-gritty details, let me explain to you what is happening here. These

144,000 people are male Jewish virgins (Rev. 14:4). They will be hand selected by Jesus Christ, who will take them to an ancient city known as Petra, which is around one hundred miles or so outside of Jerusalem. There they will learn the art of evangelism from Jesus Christ. Then they will be set loose upon the earth to witness to as many as they can of Jesus Christ and, Lord willing, get tens of millions of people saved. Perhaps you may even be among the fortunate ones who will be personally witnessed to by one of these newly made evangelists. But because of the edicts of the Antichrist, the Jewish evangelists will be martyred like anyone else who dares to proclaim their Christianity and faith in Jesus Christ during the Tribulation.

Now that we've examined the seven seals and what will transpire as a result of them being opened, we will next look at the seven trumpets. Unfortunately things are not going to get any better.

Chapter 14
THE SEVEN TRUMPETS

R EVELATION 8 OPENS up with seven angels standing before God. Each of them is given a trumpet. As soon as they have received their trumpets, another angel is seen holding a golden censer (an ancient incense burner). The incense symbolically represents the prayers of all the born-again Christians who are alive during your day and age. This shows that even though the Christian church age will end, God will not abandon His children. He will still listen to their prayers and answer them. Proof of this can be found in verse 5—the angel takes the golden censer and throws it to the earth. Then there are noises, thunder, lightning, and an earthquake. God is now about to avenge His children.

THE FIRST TRUMPET

When the first angel sounds his trumpet, hail and fire mixed with blood begin bombarding the earth. There is so much destruction that one-third of all the trees and grass on the earth are burned up. This will greatly affect the food shortage that is already occurring throughout the world. Consider a third of the fruit trees being destroyed with fire. How much greater will the food shortage be?

As I am writing this book, there have been dozens of wildfires in the United States over the past few months,

burning hundreds of thousands of acres.[1] There are wildfires burning in other countries around the world as well.
Some of those fires have been so huge and horrific that
it looks like a scene from Dante's *Inferno* is being played
out. During the Tribulation there will be fires burning in
multiple locations around the world until a third of all the
trees and grass are destroyed. Surely it will look as if the
earth was suddenly plunged into the bowels of hell.

THE SECOND TRUMPET

When the second angel sounds his trumpet, "something
like a great mountain, burning with fire, was thrown into
the sea. A third of the sea became blood, a third of the
living creatures in the sea died, and a third of the ships
were destroyed" (Rev. 8:8–9).

The apostle John had never seen a comet, meteor, or
asteroid strike the earth, which is why he used what language he could to best describe what he was witnessing.
Nowadays we know what John witnessed was most likely
a celestial body striking the earth. Any sizable comet,
meteor, or asteroid that strikes the sea will cause global
destruction on a scale we've never seen before. In the
United States alone around half of the population lives
in coastal areas.[2] More than a billion people worldwide
live in low-lying coastal areas.[3] Now imagine tsunamis
hundreds of feet tall striking the coastlines of the world.
Think of the death toll that will result from such massive
tsunamis striking the coastlines.

In addition to the human death toll, Revelation 8 tells
us that one-third of all sea life will die and one-third of all
sailing vessels will be destroyed. The earth, already facing
a global famine of epic proportions, will now face even

greater famine as one-third of all the fish will be dead. We know that at the very least one-fourth of the world's population perished as a result of the seven seals. We can expect that as many as hundreds of millions more will perish as a result of the tsunami caused by the second trumpet.

THE THIRD TRUMPET

Once the third angel blows his trumpet, "a great star from heaven, burning like a torch, fell on a third of the rivers and on the springs of waters" (Rev. 8:10). The last burning object that fell from heaven destroyed a third of the fish in the sea—that is the salt water of the world. Now a third of the fresh water will be affected by the next burning object. The great star is called Wormwood, and many people will die because they drank bitter water contaminated by Wormwood.

THE FOURTH TRUMPET

When the fourth trumpet sounds, a third of the sun, moon, and stars will lose their ability to shine as bright as they normally should (Rev. 8:12). Because the heavenly objects lose a third of their luminosity, the daytime will be a third darker than normal, and the nighttime will even be darker. Before the fifth trumpet sounds, we are forewarned that the next trumpets will be even worse. An angel flies through heaven, saying, "Woe, woe, woe to the inhabitants of the earth, because of the other trumpet blasts of the three angels, who are yet to sound!" (Rev. 8:13).

The Fifth Trumpet

Revelation 9:1–12 describes a horrific scene that will play out in your time. An angel will descend from heaven and open the bottomless pit. Once he does, great billowing smoke will be released that will darken the sun even more and make the atmosphere dark as well. Locust-like creatures with a fearsome appearance will emerge out of the bottomless pit. They will have stingers like scorpions and will be able to torment those without the seal of God on their foreheads for five months. People who are born-again Christians at that point will not be touched or tormented by the creatures. The torment everyone else will face is so great that they will try to kill themselves, but they won't be able to. Verse 6 clearly points that out: "In those days men will seek death but will not find it. They will desire to die, but death will elude them." Death will be temporarily suspended for those five months of agony and torment.

The Sixth Trumpet

When the sixth trumpet is sounded, a great war will take place (Rev. 9:13–21). An army of two hundred million will be unleashed. However, this will not be an army made up of human beings. This army will be a demonic one. Let's take a moment to look at the description of this army.

This army of demonic horsemen have breastplates of "fiery red, hyacinth blue, and sulfur yellow." The horses have heads that look like the heads of lions, and their mouths spew fire, smoke, and brimstone (Rev. 9:17). This is definitely not a human army. This demonic army will probably ascend from the bottomless pit after the locust-like creatures have been released, but this army won't appear until at least five months later. The end result of this army's appearance will be the death of one-third of mankind (Rev. 9:18). If you'll remember, one-fourth of mankind was already killed when the fourth seal was broken. If the earth's population is about eight billion during the Tribulation, then two billion will die as a result of the events related to the fourth seal, bringing the population down to six billion. With the unleashing of this demonic army, another third of the population will die, around two billion, bringing the population down to four million. In other words, even before we reach the midway point of the Tribulation, half of the world's total population will die! Just as He did during the ten plagues of Egypt when Moses confronted Pharaoh, God will try to get everyone's attention and let them know they must repent of their sins and get saved before it's too late. But how many will listen?

THE SEVEN THUNDERS AND THE TWO WITNESSES

Before the seventh trumpet is sounded, an interlude happens. I don't know how long this interlude will last, but it won't last for long. Before the seventh trumpet is blown, two other major events occur. Revelation 10:3 tells us that there are seven thunders. As the apostle John was about to write down and reveal what the seven thunders were, he heard a voice that told him not to write down and reveal what he had just seen—the seven thunders were to be sealed and remain a complete mystery until the time they sound. No one can honestly tell you what the seven thunders are or what will happen when they're released. All I can tell you is that according to the pattern, they could very well be seven more judgments the earth will have to face. If you are living after the seven thunders sounded, you may know what each thunder entailed better than I ever could. But for now let's look at what we do know will happen.

During the time of the sixth trumpet, the Jewish Temple will be rebuilt. This is commonly referred to as the Third Temple. The Second Temple was standing when Christ was around, but it was destroyed in AD 70. During the Tribulation you will probably hear about or see on television or the Internet the reconstruction of the Jewish Temple on the Temple Mount in Jerusalem. Once the reconstruction is finished, two witnesses sent from God will appear in Jerusalem and preach of God and salvation through Jesus Christ for forty-two months, or three and a half years (Rev. 11:3). This will cause a lot of people to become furious—especially the Antichrist, since he is trying to set up his new world order under his personal dictatorship. It's easy to assume that the Antichrist will not want any competition. But for three and a half years he won't be able to do anything about it, try as he may.

Anyone who tries to hurt the two witnesses will be destroyed by fire that will proceed out of their mouths (Rev. 11:5). This power given to the two witnesses to defend themselves obviously can only be a supernatural occurrence. Yet destroying their enemies with fire is not the only miracle that the two witnesses will be able to perform. The two witnesses will also be able to stop it from raining, turn water into blood, and strike the earth will all manner of plagues (Rev. 11:6).

Once the two witnesses finish their three and a half years of witnessing and testifying of Jesus Christ and His gift of eternal salvation, they will be killed by another demonic creature that will rise out of the bottomless pit. This creature is referred to as "the beast," which could be a direct reference to the Antichrist himself (Rev. 11:7).

The bodies of the two witnesses will lie in the street of Jerusalem for three and a half days, and people will rejoice over their deaths because the two prophets tormented those who dwell on the earth during their three and a half years of testimony. However, at the end of three and a half days God will resurrect them and "great fear" will fall on those who see them. God will then call them up to heaven. They will physically ascend to heaven in a cloud while their enemies watch. Once the two witnesses are taken up, a great earthquake will destroy a tenth of the city of Jerusalem, killing seven thousand people (Rev. 11:8–13).

THE SEVENTH TRUMPET

When an angel sounds the seventh trumpet, it proclaims a time of triumph: "The kingdoms of the world have become the kingdoms of our Lord, and of His Christ, and He shall reign forever and ever" (Rev. 11:15). The twenty-four elders, who were sitting on their thrones, now fall down on their faces and worship God, saying, "We give You thanks, O Lord God Almighty, who is and was and who is to come, because You have taken Your great power and begun to reign" (Rev. 11:17). But it must be remembered that the seventh trumpet is also the third woe (Rev. 11:14). Further judgment is ushered in with the sounding of the seventh trumpet, including lightning, noises, thundering, an earthquake, and great hail (Rev. 11:19). And the worst is yet to come.

THE TIMELINE

We started our Tribulation with the seven seals. Now we can add the seven trumpets.

- The first seal—A man of peace will arrive and seemingly solve all the problems of the world. He is identified in the Bible as the Antichrist.

- The second seal—Wars will suddenly break out, possibly around most of the world.

- The third seal—Currencies from around the world will become worthless due in part to hyperinflation. A global famine will occur, and a person will have to work a full day to make enough money to buy a loaf of bread.

- The fourth seal—One-fourth of the world's population (around two billion people) will be killed by war, famine, and wild animals. Many will end up in hell because they did not get saved when they had the chance.

- The fifth seal—People will end up as martyrs because they became born-again Christians. They will be killed, but they will go to heaven rather than hell.

- The sixth seal—A great earthquake will happen. The sun will turn black. The moon will turn red. The stars of heaven will fall. The heavens will be rolled back like a scroll.

Every mountain and island will be moved out of its normal position.

- The seventh seal—Nothing will happen that has an immediate or physical effect upon you or the earth.

- The first trumpet—Hail and fire will destroy one-third of the trees and grass.

- The second trumpet—A comet, meteor, or asteroid will strike the sea, killing a third of the living creatures in the sea, destroying a third of the ships, and creating massive tsunamis that will kill millions of people around the world.

- The third trumpet—Another comet, meteor, or asteroid will strike the fresh water of the world, and one-third of the fresh water will become poisonous. Many will die as a result.

- The fourth trumpet—The sun, moon, and stars will lose one-third of their luminosity, and the earth will become one-third darker during both the daytime and nighttime as a result.

- The fifth trumpet—Demonic, locust-like creatures will torment people without the seal of God on their foreheads for five months.

- The sixth trumpet—A demonic army of two hundred million will be let loose upon the

earth and one-third of the earth's population will die as a result.

- The seven thunders—We do not know what
  will happen when the seven thunders sound.
  It is likely they will entail more judgments.

- The two witnesses—After the Temple is
  rebuilt, the two witnesses will appear for
  three and a half years. They will testify of
  Jesus Christ and His salvation and be able to
  perform signs and wonders, including stopping the rain, turning water to blood, and
  striking the earth with plagues. They will be
  killed by the beast, be resurrected after three
  and a half days, and ascend to heaven in full
  view of their enemies.

- The seventh trumpet—Recognition of God
  and His triumph will take place in heaven,
  but there will also be further judgments
  upon the earth. We also find out that the
  worst is still yet to come.

I can only pray that if you're living at this point of time
in the Tribulation, you have decided to become a born-
again Christian. God doesn't want you to die and end up
in hell. That's why He is having me write this book, so He
can still reach out to you during the Tribulation. He wants
you to get saved so that one day soon you can join all of us
in heaven. But your final destination is entirely up to you.
If you haven't been saved yet by becoming a born-again
Christian, please do so now. Please choose Christ now

while you still have some time left, because if you're living in the Tribulation at this time, then you have very little time left. More things are about to hit the earth shortly.

Chapter 15
THE ARRIVAL OF THE ANTICHRIST
AND THE FALSE PROPHET

REVELATION 13:1 INFORMS us that a beast will rise "out of the sea, having seven heads and ten horns, with ten crowns on his horns, and blasphemous names on his heads." Obviously there is a lot of symbolism here, and as we go through Revelation 13 we will come across a whole lot more.

THE ANTICHRIST

The beast that rises out of the sea is the Antichrist. The sea represents the nations of the world. The seven heads symbolically refer to seven kings and to paganism—occult practices and those who practice them. The seven heads also refer to the place where the greatest concentration of paganism will be found in the Tribulation—the city of Rome, in particular the portion of the city where the Vatican is. Revelation 17:9 explains to us that the seven heads are seven mountains (hills). There is only one place geographically where you can find seven hills that are around a major religious center—Rome and Vatican City, the home of Roman Catholicism and the seat of the pope.

The Book of Revelation also explains that of the seven kings represented by the seven heads, "five have fallen, one is, [and] the other has not yet come" (17:10). These kings represent world empires. The five that had already fallen when John was writing the Book of Revelation were the Egyptian, Assyrian, Babylonian, Medo-Persian, and Greek Empires. The Roman Empire was the one that was in existence when John was writing. The one that "has not yet come" refers to the final world empire out of which the Antichrist will arise. (See Daniel 7:2–8 for more about some of these kings and empires.)

The ten horns symbolize ten kings who will form a coalition but will eventually give their power and authority to the Antichrist (the beast).

From Revelation 13:2 we find out that the dragon (Satan) will give the beast (the Antichrist) his power, his throne, and his authority. So the Antichrist will not come upon the world scene through his own power but instead will be empowered by Satan. However, something along the way will go terribly wrong because one of the heads of the beast will be mortally wounded. It is a common belief that this represents a successful assassination attempt that results in the apparent death of the Antichrist. If this is the case, then something miraculous happens next because the "deadly wound" will be healed and the world will marvel at the beast (the Antichrist) for seemingly being able to resurrect himself (Rev. 13:3). This will be a false resurrection. Satan does not have the power to grant anyone life. That power is reserved for God and God alone. What probably will happen is the Antichrist will be proclaimed dead, but a day or so later it will be reported that he came back to life through his own power. The world will fall for this deception and worship both the dragon who gave the beast his power and the beast, saying, "Who is like the beast? Who is able to wage war with him?" (Rev.

13:4). The world is actually going to think the Antichrist is the Messiah.

For the next forty-two months (three and a half years) the Antichrist will wage war against those who are saved, the born-again Christians, and begin his reign of terror over them that will result in countless martyrdoms. He will also have power over the rest of the inhabitants of the earth (Rev. 13:5–7).

THE FALSE PROPHET

Another beast will appear on the scene. This second beast will have the same power that the first beast, the Antichrist, has. However, the Antichrist is a political figure while the second beast is a religious one. The second beast is later discovered to come from that major religious center that has seven hills around it (Rev. 17:9), which we have already identified as Vatican City. This means that the second beast will be the pope during the Tribulation. This makes perfect sense, since many tenets of Roman Catholicism are based on ancient pagan religions and practices.

The second beast, referred to later in Revelation as the false prophet, will be able to perform many apparent miracles. One of those miracles is that he will be able to make "fire come down from heaven on the earth in the sight of men" (Rev. 13:13). However, the false prophet will not do this for personal glory; he will do it so he can lead the world into worshipping the Antichrist (Rev. 13:12). The false prophet will instruct the people of the world to erect an image to the Antichrist. Once this statue is complete, the false prophet will endow it with life and the statue will then be able to speak. Those who do not worship this image of the Antichrist will be killed (Rev. 13:14–15).

THE MARK OF THE BEAST

Once the Antichrist is being lauded as the Messiah and worshipped, the false prophet will cause everyone on the earth "to receive a mark on their right hand or on their forehead" (Rev. 13:16). The mark will be in one of three forms: a mark (or the logo of the Antichrist), the name of the beast (the name of the Antichrist), or the number of his name, which is 666 (Rev. 13:17–18).

When people receive the mark of the beast, it will be placed "in" their right hands or their foreheads (Rev. 13:16, KJV). This mark could be a computer chip implanted underneath the skin, referred to as an implant chip or an RFID chip. In fact, early versions of these chips are being used among many volunteers right now in order to determine if they work as well as has been projected.[1] Those who have them now will simply hold their hand up to a scanner, and it will do things such as unlock security doors at their workplaces or homes. Eventually these chips will be perfected to such a degree that people will be able to buy and sell things with these implanted chips, similar to the chips that are now in credit and debit cards.

However, having such a chip implanted will come with a very heavy price and dire consequences. The people who take the mark of the beast will receive eternal condemnation from God (Rev. 14:9–11). Christians will not take the mark of the beast. Many will be martyred as a result, but they will receive their eternal reward in heaven. Psalm 84:10 says, "I had rather be a doorkeeper in the house of my God than to dwell in the tents of wickedness." I would have to agree. There is no comparison between heaven and hell. So when faced with the decision whether or not to take the mark of the beast, choose wisely. Your decision will have eternal consequences.

BABYLON

Before we move on to the seven bowls, we need to discuss one other entity described in Revelation—Babylon. In the Bible, Babylon is often associated with sin and pride. Revelation 17 and 18 provide a better understanding of what Babylon truly stands for. The Babylon mentioned in Revelation is actually a spiritual Babylon; in other words, *Babylon* refers to the beliefs and religious practices of the people of the ancient city of Babylon, which existed around five thousand years ago. Revelation 18:23 tells us that the religious practice of this spiritual Babylon in your day and age is sorcery, or witchcraft. The same verse also states that "all nations" of the world are going to be deceived by this occult religious system.

The symbol of Babylon in Revelation 17 and 18 is a woman named Mystery. According to Scripture, she is "the mother of prostitutes and of the abominations of the earth" (Rev. 17:5). This prostitute will ride on the beast (the Antichrist). The prostitute is also symbolic of the occult religion that comes from the Vatican. Because she rides on the beast, she is riding on the Antichrist's coattails; she is successful in pushing occult religion to the forefront because of his success with the masses. Both Babylon and the Antichrist will be destroyed once and for all at the end of the Tribulation. If you can find a Bible, I strongly suggest you read the Book of Revelation from beginning to end; when you get to chapters 17 and 18, you will see what will befall the prostitute (Babylon) and the Antichrist.

Chapter 16

THE SEVEN BOWLS AND THE BATTLE OF ARMAGEDDON

A	s THE TRIBULATION continues, seven angels will be given seven bowls (or vials). They have the last seven plagues, "for in them the wrath of God is complete" (Rev. 15:1). The golden bowls given to the seven angels are "full of the wrath of God," and the angels are told to pour them out on the earth (Rev. 15:7; 16:1).

THE FIRST BOWL

When an angel pours out the first bowl on the earth, "foul and grievous sores" appear on the people "who had the mark of the beast and those who worshipped his image" (Rev. 16:2). No born-again Christian who is alive when this event happens will be touched by it. They have the mark of God on them, they are saved, and God determined they would be spared from His wrath. Jesus Christ already paid the price for them.

THE SECOND BOWL

The second angel appears and pours out his bowl on the earth (Rev. 16:3). This bowl turns all of the water in the sea into blood, and every living creature in the sea will die. Once again, millions of people will die. The worldwide famine that has been going on for years will become even worse.

THE THIRD BOWL

The third angel descends and pours out another bowl on the earth (Rev. 16:4). This time all of the fresh water in the world will be turned into blood. On top of the global famine that is running rampant, there will now be no more fresh water in rivers, lakes, ponds, or other natural fresh water sources. The only fresh water left will be stored or bottled water. Countless people will die of dehydration within three to four days. The catastrophes will only get worse.

THE FOURTH BOWL

When the fourth angel appears, instead of pouring out his bowl on the earth, he pours it out on the sun (Rev. 16:8–9). The result is that men will be scorched with fire. This could very well be because of a massive coronal mass ejection. A coronal mass ejection (CME) is when the sun shoots out a massive amount of its own energy in the form of plasma. As previously stated, it has been predicted that a sizable CME could destroy the electrical grids around the world. That kind of sudden energy surge would burn out every single transformer and power plant in the world.

The truly sad thing about this event, when people will be scorched with great heat, is that it will cause people to blaspheme God rather than repent and give Him glory (Rev. 16:9). God is trying to get everyone's attention by using these events to prove that He and He alone is God, not that so-called Messianic figure, the Antichrist. If the

Antichrist were truly the Messiah, he would be able to stop all the plagues and punishments that have been going on for years. But you should know by now that he hasn't been able to do a thing to stop any of these divine judgments. He is powerless in the face of God! If you're not saved yet, then you need to switch sides, because the one you're on right now can do nothing to stand up against the one true God. Choose NOW whom you will serve! The reign of the Antichrist is swiftly coming to an end. Do you want to go down with him, or do you want to end up in heaven with Jesus Christ with me and my other brothers and sisters? Make the decision now—time has almost run out for you and everyone else.

THE FIFTH BOWL

The fifth angel then appears and pours out his bowl. This bowl is poured out "on the throne of the beast [the Antichrist]" (Rev. 16:10). The *throne of the beast* refers to the headquarters of the Antichrist, the place from where he will be operating his global kingdom. Based on what the Scriptures have taught me, I believe the location of the Antichrist's headquarters is probably Jerusalem. Whether or not I'm correct doesn't really matter. What does matter is that the entire area where the Antichrist resides will be thrown into darkness. There also appears to be an element of physical pain involved with the fifth bowl judgment because the Bible says, "They gnawed their tongues because of the anguish, and blasphemed the God of heaven because of their pains and their sores" (Rev. 16:10–11).

What is even more heartbreaking to me is that mankind will continue to blaspheme or curse God because of the pain they're in. Even in the face of the wrath of God, they still will not repent of their deeds.

THE SIXTH BOWL

We learn in Revelation 16:12 that the sixth angel pours out his bowl on the Euphrates River, which completely dries up. Then we find out why: "to prepare the way for the kings from the East" (Rev. 16:12).

Toward the end of your time, not everyone is going to be worshipping the Antichrist. In fact, somewhere in the East an army made up of one nation or many nations will be able to march over and beyond the Euphrates River to go against the armies of the Antichrist in a place where the Valley of Jehoshaphat used to be located. (See Joel 3:2.) This place is now known as Megiddo or Armageddon. You may have heard of this place. It is where the final battle will begin.

THE SEVENTH BOWL

When the seventh angel appears, he pours out his bowl into the air. Once he does, a loud voice comes out of the temple of heaven, from the throne, and proclaims, "It is done!" (Rev. 16:17). Immediately after that happens, the world's strongest earthquake hits and "the great city" (probably Jerusalem) is divided into three sections. Next, the great city of Babylon (Vatican City, more than likely) is completely destroyed. Probably due to the great earthquake, every island will flee and every mountain will be brought down (Rev. 16:18–20).

Great hailstones weighing around one hundred pounds will fall out of heaven upon mankind. Imagine a hailstone of that size suddenly striking someone. That person is going to be either severely hurt or dead. Those are the only options when an object with that much weight strikes someone with such velocity behind it. Millions upon millions of them will strike the whole earth. And still, unrepentant mankind will blaspheme God.

THE TIMELINE

For one last time let's take a look at the timeline of events you should be watching for during the Tribulation with the addition of the events of the seven bowls.

- The first seal—A man of peace will arrive and seemingly solve all the problems of the world. He is identified in the Bible as the Antichrist.

- The second seal—Wars will suddenly break out, possibly around most of the world.

- The third seal—Currencies from around the world will become worthless due in part to hyperinflation. A global famine will occur, and a person will have to work a full day to make enough money to buy a loaf of bread.

- The fourth seal—One-fourth of the world's population (around two billion people) will be killed by war, famine, and wild animals. Many will end up in hell because they did not get saved when they had the chance.

- The fifth seal—People will end up as martyrs because they became born-again Christians.

They will be killed, but they will go to heaven rather than hell.

- The sixth seal—A great earthquake will happen. The sun will turn black. The moon will turn red. The stars of heaven will fall. The heavens will be rolled back like a scroll. Every mountain and island will be moved out of its normal position.

- The seventh seal—Nothing will happen that has an immediate or physical effect upon you or the earth.

- The first trumpet—Hail and fire will destroy one-third of the trees and grass.

- The second trumpet—A comet, meteor, or asteroid will strike the sea, killing a third of the living creatures in the sea, destroying a third of the ships, and creating massive tsunamis that will kill millions of people around the world.

- The third trumpet—Another comet, meteor, or asteroid will strike the fresh water of the world, and one-third of the fresh water will become poisonous. Many will die as a result.

- The fourth trumpet—The sun, moon, and stars will lose one-third of their luminosity, and the earth will become one-third darker during both the daytime and nighttime as a result.

- The fifth trumpet—Demonic, locust-like
  creatures will torment people without
  the seal of God on their foreheads for
  five months.

- The sixth trumpet—A demonic army of two
  hundred million will be let loose upon the
  earth, and one-third of the earth's population will die as a result.

- The seven thunders—We do not know what
  will happen when the seven thunders sound.
  It is likely they will entail more judgments.

- The two witnesses—After the Temple is
  rebuilt, the two witnesses will appear for
  three and a half years. They will testify of
  Jesus Christ and His salvation and be able to
  perform signs and wonders, including stopping the rain, turning water to blood, and
  striking the earth with plagues. They will be
  killed by the beast, be resurrected after three
  and a half days, and ascend to heaven in full
  view of their enemies.

- The seventh trumpet—Recognition of God
  and His triumph will take place in heaven,
  but there will also be further judgments
  upon the earth. We also find out that the
  worst is still yet to come.

- The first bowl—Great sores will
  strike mankind.

- The second bowl—The sea will turn into blood. All sea creatures will die.

- The third bowl—All fresh water will turn into blood.

- The fourth bowl—Mankind will be scorched by the sun.

- The fifth bowl—The throne of the beast (probably Jerusalem) will be thrust into darkness. Those living there will be physically affected by the great darkness.

- The sixth bowl—The Euphrates River will dry up.

- The seventh bowl—The greatest earthquake in the history of the world will occur. Giant hailstones will strike mankind around the world.

After the seventh bowl is poured out, there will be very little time left. The end is near, and only a few more things will happen before the final event, known as the Battle of Armageddon. When the Battle of Armageddon begins, the Antichrist will join all of his armies together and march against Jerusalem to destroy God's people once and for all. However, something will happen that prevents the destruction of Israel. Let's take a look at it in the apostle John's own words:

> I saw heaven opened. And there was a white horse.
> He who sat on it is called Faithful and True, and
> in righteousness He judges and wages war. His eyes

are like a flame of fire, and on His head are many crowns. He has a name written, that no one knows but He Himself. He is clothed with a robe dipped in blood. His name is called The Word of God. The armies in heaven, clothed in fine linen, white and clean, followed Him on white horses. Out of His mouth proceeds a sharp sword, with which He may strike the nations. "He shall rule them with an iron scepter." He treads the winepress of the fury and wrath of God the Almighty. On His robe and on His thigh He has a name written: KING OF KINGS AND LORD OF LORDS.

—REVELATION 19:11–16

This will be the Second Coming of Jesus Christ. There will be armies descending with Him from out of heaven. Note that there is more than one army with Him. The armies will be made up of the angelic host of heaven (angels) and the church (all the people who were saved). The Antichrist will have gathered all the armies of the earth together to foolishly try to contend with their Maker but to no avail. The Battle of Armageddon will be over soon after it has begun. The Antichrist and the false prophet will be taken from the battlefield and thrown into the lake of fire, where they shall remain eternally (Rev. 19:19–21).

Satan will be bound up and thrown into the bottomless pit for a thousand years and then released for a small season. Jesus Christ will reign on the earth for one thousand years, what is known as the millennial reign of Christ. We will reign and live with Him during those thousand years. Once this period of time is over, the final judgment of Jesus Christ will happen. All those who are in hell will face Jesus Christ one by one at His throne and be condemned to the lake of fire for all of eternity for rejecting His payment for their sins. They must pay for their sins in the lake of fire.

There's a lot more to all of these events, but I am running out of space. But before ending this book, let me implore you one last time to become a born-again Christian. The choice to enter into heaven or hell is yours. You get to choose your final destination, and you will have to live with your decision for eternity. If you haven't made that decision yet, please go back to chapter 10 and reread it. Your eternal existence depends on you making the correct decision. However, if you still aren't ready to make such a decision, remember you can make that decision at any moment. But I can't guarantee that you'll always have access to this book. If you're living during the Tribulation, the Bible and any books related to it will be marked for destruction. I believe that since you found this book, there will be other such Bible-based books around. God wanted you to find this book so you could get saved. Think about that most carefully. Even in the midst of all of the chaos and turmoil you're living through right now because of the Antichrist and his forces, God is still trying to find a way to get your attention so He can tell you about the choice you have to make: heaven or hell. Choose now, for if you die before you make a choice, you will have chosen hell. You will die without Jesus Christ, and your eternity will be spent in the lake of fire. Please, choose now while you can.

I leave you with this passage from the Bible:

> The LORD bless you and keep you; the LORD make
> His face to shine upon you, and be gracious unto

you; the LORD lift His countenance upon you, and give you peace.

—NUMBERS 6:24–26

To God's born-again children and to God Himself, I leave these verses from the Bible:

Now to Him who is able to keep you from falling and to present you blameless before the presence of His glory with rejoicing, to the only wise God our Savior, be glory and majesty, dominion and power, both now and forever. Amen.

—JUDE 24–25

NOTES

Chapter 1
The Definition of *Rapture* and Its Historical Usages

1. Blue Letter Bible, s.v. "*harpazo*," accessed March 14, 2017, https://www.blueletterbible.org/lang/lexicon/lexicon .cfm?Strongs=G726&t=KJV.
2. Margaret MacDonald, "The Handwritten Account by Margaret MacDonald of Her Vision," in Tim LaHaye, *The Rapture: Who Will Face the Tribulation?* (Eugene, OR: Harvest House, 2016), 245.
3. C. I. Scofield, ed., *Scofield Reference Bible* (London: Oxford University Press, 1909).
4. William E. Blackstone, *Jesus Is Coming* (Chicago: F. H. Revell, 1878).
5. Charles Kingsley, *Hereward the Wake* (London: Macmillan and Co., 1866).
6. John Gill, *An Exposition of the New Testament* (London: W. H. Collingridge, 1748).
7. John Milton, "Paradise Lost" (Chicago: W. B. Conkey Co., 1800), Book 11, line 706. Originally published in 1667.
8. John Guillim, *A Display of Heraldrie* (London: T. R., 1660). Originally published in 1610.
9. William Bonde, *The Pylgrimage of Perfection* (London: Richarde Pynson, 1526).
10. Ranulphus Higden, *Polychronicon*, ed. Churchill Babington, trans. John Trevisa (London: Longman & Co., 1865). Written c. 1342.
11. John Lydgate, *Auncient Historie and Onely Trewe and Syncere Chronicle of the Warres Betwixte the Grecians and the Troyans* (London: Thomas Marshe, 1555). Written 1412–1420.
12. *The Vernon Manuscript* (Cambridge: D. S. Brewer, 1987). Written c. 1400.
13. *Biblia Sacra Vulgata* (Basileae: Thomas Guarinius, 1578), 1 Thessalonians 4:17. Originally translated in 405.

CHAPTER 2
THE HISTORICAL CONCEPT OF THE
PRE-TRIBULATION RAPTURE

1. Thomas Scott, *The Works of the Late Rev. Thomas Scott*, Vol. 4, ed. John Scott (London: L. B. Seeley and Son, 1823). First twenty sermons were originally published in 1796.
2. James Macknight, *A Harmony of the Four Gospels, Vol. 2* (London: Longman, Hurst, Rees, and Orme, 1809). Originally published in 1763.
3. Gill, *An Exposition of the New Testament*.
4. Morgan Edwards, *Two Academical Exercises on Subjects Bearing the Following Titles; Millennium, Last-Novelties* (Philadelphia: Dobson and Lang, 1788). Originally written in 1744.
5. Philip Doddridge, *The Family Expositor* (London: John Wilson, 1739).
6. Peter Jurieu, *The Accomplishment of the Scripture Prophecies* (London: n.p., 1687).
7. "Ephraem the Syrian," JoshuaNet, from Grant R. Jeffrey, *Final Warning* (Eugene, OR: Harvest House, 1996), accessed May 15, 2017, http://joshuanet.org/articles/ephraem1.htm.
8. Victorinus, *The Sacred Writings of Victorinus (Annotated Edition)* (Altenmünster, Germany: Jazzybee Verlag Jürgen Beck, 2012).
9. "What Did Ancient Church Fathers Believe About the Rapture?," *Beginning and End* (blog), August 2, 2013, accessed May 15, 2017, http://beginningandend.com/what-did-ancient-church-fathers-believe-about-the-rapture/.
10. Ibid.
11. *The Westminster Dictionary of Church History*, ed. Jerald Brauer, s.v. "Ignatius" (Philadelphia: Westminster, 1971); David Hugh Farmer, *The Oxford Dictionary of the Saints*, s.v. "Ignatius of Antioch" (New York: Oxford University Press, 1987).
12. Thomas Ice, "A Brief History of the Rapture," *Believer's Web* (blog), June 6, 2006, accessed May 15, 2017, http://www.believersweb.org/view.cfm?id=1141&rc=1&list=multi.
13. David K. Hebert, "The Rapture of the Church: A Doctrine of the Early Church or a Recent Development of the

Dispensational Movement?," accessed May 15, 2017, http://
web.oru.edu/current_students/class_pages/grtheo/mmankins
/DrHebert/M.A.%20Thesis/MA(Th)%20Thesis.CH-3e%20
Indirect%20Ref%20to%20Rapture%20by%20Fathers.pdf.

CHAPTER 3
BIBLICAL EXAMPLES OF RAPTURES

1. Library Index, "Murrain," accessed March 31, 2017, https://
   www.libraryindex.com/encyclopedia/pages/cpxlf410ry
   /murrain-cattle-disease-animals.html.
2. Blue Letter Bible, s.v. "*laqach*," accessed May 8, 2017, https://
   www.blueletterbible.org/lang/lexicon/lexicon.cfm?Strongs
   =H3947&t=KJV.
3. Ibid.

CHAPTER 4
THE PROPHETIC MARKER

1. American-Israeli Cooperative Enterprise, "History: Timeline
   for the History of Judaism," Jewish Virtual Library, accessed
   April 4, 2017, http://www.jewishvirtuallibrary.org/timeline
   -for-the-history-of-judaism.
2. Ibid.
3. Ibid.
4. "Cyrus the Great," Livius.org, last modified January 12, 2017,
   accessed April 4, 2017, http://www.livius.org/articles/person
   /cyrus-the-great/cyrus-takes-babylon/.
5. "Alexander Defeats the Persians, 331 BC," Ibis Communi-
   cations Inc., EyeWitness to History, 2000, accessed April 4,
   2017, http://www.eyewitnesstohistory.com/alexander.htm.
6. American-Israeli Cooperative Enterprise, "Ancient Jewish
   History: The Greeks and the Jews," Jewish Virtual Library,
   accessed April 4, 2017, http://www.jewishvirtuallibrary.org
   /the-ancient-greeks-and-the-jews-jewish-virtual-library.
7. American-Israeli Cooperative Enterprise, "The Maccabees/
   Hasmoneans: History and Overview (166–129 BCE)," Jewish
   Virtual Library, accessed April 4, 2017, http://www.jewish
   virtuallibrary.org/jsource/History/Maccabees.html.
8. "Jews in Roman Times," PBS.org, accessed April 4, 2017,
   http://www.pbs.org/empires/romans/empire/jews.html.

9. American-Israeli Cooperative Enterprise, "Ancient Jewish History: Roman Rule (63 BCE–313 CE)," Jewish Virtual Library, accessed April 4, 2017, http://www.jewish virtuallibrary.org/roman-rule-63bce-313ce.

10. "Herod Antipas," *Encyclopædia Britannica*, accessed April 4, 2017, https://www.britannica.com/biography/Herod-Antipas.

11. G. J. Goldberg, "Chronology of the War According to Josephus Part 7: The Siege and Destruction of Jerusalem, March 70–September 70," Josephus.org, accessed April 4, 2017, http://www.josephus.org/FlJosephus2/warChronology7Fall .html.

12. "Titus Flavius Sabinus Vespasianus (AD 40–81)," Illustrated History of the Roman Empire, accessed April 4, 2017, http:// www.roman-empire.net/emperors/titus.html.

13. Sarina Roffé, "Jews Built Roman Coliseum After Destruction of Second Temple," Sephardic Genealogy Resources, accessed April 4, 2017, http://www.jewishgen.org/Sephardic/coliseum .htm.

14. Lambert Dolphin, "The Destruction of the Second Temple," TempleMount.org, accessed April 4, 2017, http://www.temple mount.org/destruct2.html.

15. "Emperor Titus: The Man Who Destroyed the Temple," Go Jerusalem, accessed April 4, 2017, http://www.gojerusalem .com/article/301/Emperor-Titus--The-Man-Who-Destroyed -the-Temple/.

16. Dolphin, "The Destruction of the Second Temple."

17. Walid Ahmed Khalidi et al., "Palestine," *Encyclopædia Britannica*, last updated May 12, 2017, accessed June 6, 2017, https://www.britannica.com/place/Palestine.

18. "Jews in the Land of Israel (636–1880 CE)," Israel Ministry of Foreign Affairs, accessed April 4, 2017, http://www.mfa.gov.il /MFA/AboutIsrael/Maps/Pages/Jewish%20Communities%20 in%20the%20Land%20of%20Israel%20-7th-11th.aspx.

19. Stewart Mills, "Population and Area of Ottoman and British Mandate Palestine and Israel," *Historic Population of Israel/ Palestine* (blog), July 15, 2013, accessed April 4, 2017, http:// palestineisraelpopulation.blogspot.com/.

20. Theodor Herzl, *The Jewish State*, trans. Sylvie D'Avigdor (n.p.: American Zionist Emergency Council, 1946), viewed online through the Jewish Virtual Library, accessed April 4,

2017, http://www.jewishvirtuallibrary.org/quot-the-jewish
-state-quot-theodor-herzl. Originally written in 1896.

21. "Declaration of the Establishment of the State of Israel, May
14, 1948," Israel Ministry of Foreign Affairs, accessed June 6,
2017, http://www.mfa.gov.il/mfa/foreignpolicy/peace/guide
/pages/declaration%20of%20establishment%20of%20state%20
of%20israel.aspx.

22. American-Israeli Cooperative Enterprise, "Immigration
to Israel: The Second Aliyah (1904–1914)," Jewish Virtual
Library, accessed April 4, 2017, http://www.jewishvirtual
library.org/the-second-aliyah-1904-1914.

23. Ibid.; see also "Pogroms," Encyclopedia.com, accessed April
4, 2017, http://www.encyclopedia.com/history/modern
-europe/russian-soviet-and-cis-history/pogroms.

24. Dan Leon, "The Jewish National Fund: How the Land Was
'Redeemed,'" *Palestine-Israel Journal* 12, no. 4 (May 2006),
accessed April 4, 2017, http://www.pij.org/details.php?id=410.

25. American-Israeli Cooperative Enterprise, "The Kibbutz and
Moshav: History and Overview," Jewish Virtual Library,
accessed April 4, 2017, http://www.jewishvirtuallibrary.org
/jsource/Society_&_Culture/kibbutz.html.

26. Mills, "Population."

27. A&E Television Networks, LLC, "The Balfour Declaration,"
History.com, accessed April 4, 2017, http://www.history.com
/this-day-in-history/the-balfour-declaration.

28. "Mandate: League of Nations," *Encyclopædia Britannica*,
accessed April 4, 2017, https://www.britannica.com/topic
/mandate-League-of-Nations.

29. American-Israeli Cooperative Enterprise, "British Palestine
Mandate: Text of the Mandate (July 24, 1922)," Jewish Virtual Library, accessed April 4, 2017, http://www.jewish
virtuallibrary.org/text-of-the-british-mandate-for-palestine.

30. American-Israeli Cooperative Enterprise, "Pre-State Israel:
The 1936 Arab Riots (April–November 1936)" Jewish Virtual
Library, accessed April 4, 2017, http://www.jewishvirtual
library.org/the-1936-arab-riots.

31. "British White Paper of 1939," The Avalon Project, Lillian
Goldman Law Library, accessed April 4, 2017, http://avalon
.law.yale.edu/20th_century/brwh1939.asp.

32. A&E Television Networks, "This Day in History: May 14, 1948—State of Israel Proclaimed," History.com, accessed April 4, 2017, http://www.history.com/this-day-in-history /state-of-israel-proclaimed.

33. "The Arab-Israeli War of 1948," Office of the Historian, US Department of State, accessed April 4, 2017, https://history .state.gov/milestones/1945-1952/arab-israeli-war.

34. Arthur Conan Doyle, *The Adventure of the Abbey Grange*, East of the Web, accessed April 4, 2017, http://www.eastofthe web.com/short-stories/UBooks/AdveAbbe.shtml#1.

CHAPTER 5
SIGNS OF THE TIME

1. Joe Maxwell, "Camping Misses End of World," *Christianity Today*, October 24, 1994, accessed April 4, 2017, http://www .christianitytoday.com/ct/1994/october24/4tc084.html.

2. Nick Carbone, "Judgment Day? No Way! What's Behind the May 21, 2011, End-of-the-World Rumors," *Time*, May 15, 2011, accessed April 5, 2017, http://newsfeed.time.com /2011/05/15/judgment-day-no-way-what%E2%80%99s-behind -the-may-21-2011-end-of-the-world-rumors/; David Gardner, "Will Saturday Be the End of the World? Evangelicals Party Like There's No Tomorrow," *Daily Mail*, accessed June 6, 2017, http://www.dailymail.co.uk/news/article-1388972 /Judgment-Day-Rapture-Parties-planned-evangelist-Harold -Camping-predicts-huge-earthquake.html.

3. "Judgment Day Preacher Harold Camping Dies, Aged 92," *Guardian*, December 17, 2013, accessed April 5, 2017, https:// www.theguardian.com/world/2013/dec/17/preacher-harold -camping-dies-the-rapture.

4. Ibid.; see also Adelle M. Banks, "End May Be Coming for Harold Camping's Family Radio Ministry," *Huffington Post*, May 14, 2013, accessed June 6, 2017, http://www.huffington post.com/2013/05/14/end-may-be-coming-for-har_n_3274262 .html?utm_hp_ref=religion.

5. Jennifer LeClaire, "Harold Camping Admits Rapture Prediction Was 'Sinful Statement,'" *Charisma News*, March 7, 2012, accessed April 5, 2017, http://www.charismanews.com

/us/32958-harold-camping-admits-rapture-prediction-was
-sinful-statement.

CHAPTER 6
SIGNS IN THE PROPHETIC TIMELINE

1. Emma Schiller and Chloe Longhetti, "Bondi and Clo-
velly Beaches Close as Red Algae Moves In," News Limited,
November 27, 2012, accessed April 5, 2017, http://www.news
.com.au/travel/travel-updates/bondi-beach-closes-as-red
-algae-moves-in/news-story/d0e36adaa63741a8f0ea57e1ed
b43dcf.
2. "Sydney's Beaches Closed as Algae Turns the Sea Blood Red,"
The Telegraph, February 4, 2016, accessed April 5, 2017,
http://www.telegraph.co.uk/travel/destinations/oceania
/australia/galleries/Sydneys-beaches-closed-as-algae-turns
-the-sea-blood-red/.
3. Van Meguerditchian, "Beirut River Mysteriously Runs Blood
Red," *Daily Star Lebanon*, February 16, 2012, accessed April
5, 2017, http://www.dailystar.com.lb/News/Local-News/2012
/Feb-16/163449-beirut-river-mysteriously-runs-blood-red
.ashx.
4. "Blood Red Waters in Brazil!" WorldNews.com, May 10,
2015, accessed April 5, 2017, https://wn.com/blood_red_
waters_in_brazil; "The Blood Red Lake Beauty Spot Which
Is Startling Tourists in Southern France," *Daily Mail*, August
9, 2012, accessed April 5, 2017, http://www.dailymail.co.uk
/news/article-2185920/Extraordinary-natural-phenomenon
-turned-French-beauty-spot-blood-RED.html.
5. Nick Kirkpatrick, "Why Did This River in China Turn
Red?," *Washington Post*, July 29, 2014, accessed April 5, 2017,
https://www.washingtonpost.com/news/morning-mix/wp
/2014/07/29/why-did-this-river-in-china-turn-red/.
6. Sara Malm, "The River of Blood: Villagers' Shock as Slova-
kian Waterway Turns Red Overnight 'Like Something From
a Horror Film,'" *Daily Mail*, December 3, 2013, accessed
April 5, 2017, http://www.dailymail.co.uk/news/article
-2517516/The-river-blood-Villagers-shock-Slovakian-
waterway-turns-red-overnight-like-horror-film.html.

7. Elizabeth Newbern, "'Red Tide' Turns Gulf of Mexico Rust-Colored," Live Science, December 22, 2015, accessed April 5, 2017, http://www.livescience.com/53180-red-tide-gulf-of -mexico.html; Marc Lallanilla, "What Causes a Red Tide?," Live Science, March 11, 2013, accessed April 5, 2017, http:// www.livescience.com/34461-red-tide.html.

8. Jack Polden, "Biblical Scenes Filmed in China as Tens of Thousands of Toads Descend on Town Following Heavy Rainfall," *Daily Mail*, June 5, 2015, accessed April 5, 2017, http://www.dailymail.co.uk/news/article-3112207/Thousands -toads-descend-China-heavy-rainfall-results-biblical-scene .html.

9. Josh Kinney, "The Great Frog Invasion of Anderson Lake 2010," YouTube video, 0:11, August 21, 2010, accessed April 5, 2017, https://www.youtube.com/watch?v=A_9vQpWE3Ng; Josh Kinney, "The Great Frog Invasion of Anderson Lake 2010–Redux," YouTube video, 1:18, August 21, 2010, accessed April 5, 2017, https://www.youtube.com/watch?v =SYSlPe1W8XA.

10. Mike Strickland, "A Plague of Frogs—A Million Tiny Toads at Laguna Hanson, Baja," YouTube video, 1:32, June 9, 2010, accessed April 5, 2017, https://www.youtube.com /watch?v=J9UTqxQmaDw.

11. Maggie Maloney, "Mutant 'Super Lice' Outbreak Has Now Spread to Nearly Every State," *Country Living*, August 3, 2016, accessed May 12, 2017, http://www.countryliving.com /life/news/a39389/treatment-resistant-lice-outbreak/; Kyle J. Gellatly et al., "Expansion of the Knockdown Resistance Frequency Map for Human Head Lice (Phthiraptera: Pediculidae) in the United States Using Quantitative Sequencing," *Journal of Medical Entomology* 53, no. 3 (2016): 653–9, https://academic.oup.com/jme/article/53/3/653/2222496 /Expansion-of-the-Knockdown-Resistance-Frequency.

12. "'Super Lice' Outbreak Hits 25 States," Fox News Health, February 26, 2016, accessed May 12, 2017, http://www .foxnews.com/health/2016/02/26/super-lice-outbreak-hits -25-states.html.

13. Ibid.

14. Maloney, "Mutant 'Super Lice.'"

15. "Zika Virus and Complications: 2016 Public Health Emergency of International Concern," World Health Organization, accessed April 5, 2017, http://www.who.int/emergencies /zika-virus/en/; "Zika Virus," Centers for Disease Control and Prevention, accessed April 5, 2017, https://www.cdc.gov /zika/about/overview.html.

16. Mark Leberfinger, "Insect Swarms Whirl to Create Massive 'Bugnado' Vortexes Across the World," AccuWeather, June 3, 2014, accessed May 12, 2017, http://www.accuweather.com /en/weather-news/insects-swarm-like-bugnadoes/27954396.

17. "Ninety Stricken by Yamal Anthrax Outbreak—Authorities," TASS, August 2, 2016, accessed May 8, 2017, http://tass.com /society/892004.

18. "Foot-and-Mouth Outbreak of 2001," BBC News, February 18, 2011, accessed May 8, 2017, http://www.bbc.com/news/uk -england-12483017.

19. John Simkin, "Poison Gases," Spartacus Educational, September 1997, updated February 2016, accessed May 8, 2017, http://spartacus-educational.com/FWWgas.htm.

20. "All Hail Reports Near Sterling, Colorado in 2011," StormerSite, accessed April 5, 2017, http://www.stormersite.com /hail_reports/sterling_colorado/2011.

21. "Severe Weather 101—Hail Basics," The National Severe Storms Laboratory, accessed April 5, 2017, http://www.nssl .noaa.gov/education/svrwx101/hail/; Tom Steele, "How Fast Hail Falls, and Other Cold, Hard Facts," Dallas News, April 2016, accessed June 7, 2017, https://www.dallasnews.com /news/news/2016/04/12/how-fast-does-hail-fall-and-other -facts.

22. Christopher C. Burt, "World's Largest Hailstones," The Weather Company, April 30, 2011, accessed April 5, 2017, http://www.wunderground.ag/blog/weatherhistorian /comment.html?entrynum=24.

23. Scott Neuman, "Egypt's Locust Plague Threatens Israel," NPR, March 7, 2013, accessed April 5, 2017, http://www.npr .org/sections/thetwo-way/2013/03/07/173704437/egypts-locust -plague-threatens-israel.

24. Mark Tran, "Madagascar Battling Worst Locust Plague Since 1950s," Guardian, July 12, 2013, accessed April 5, 2017,

https://www.theguardian.com/global-development/2013/jul/12/madagascar-locust-plague.

25. Matthew Chance, "Locust Swarms Plague Southern Russia," CNN, August 5, 2015, accessed April 5, 2017, http://www.cnn.com/2015/08/04/europe/russia-locust-swarms/.

26. Jonathan Gilbert, "Argentina Scrambles to Fight Biggest Plague of Locusts in 60 Years," *New York Times*, January 25, 2016, accessed April 5, 2017, https://www.nytimes.com/2016/01/26/world/americas/argentina-scrambles-to-fight-biggest-plague-of-locusts-in-60-years.html?_r=0.

27. Joe Rao, "Solar Eclipses: When Is the Next One?," Space.com, April 12, 2017, accessed June 7, 2017, http://www.space.com/15584-solar-eclipses.html; "Lunar Eclipse Page," NASA, accessed June 7, 2017, https://eclipse.gsfc.nasa.gov/lunar.html.

Chapter 7
Wars and Rumors of War

1. Wayne Allyn Root, "Obama's Final Attack on Israel and the Jewish People," Fox News, January 30, 2017, accessed April 6, 2017, http://www.foxnews.com/opinion/2017/01/30/obamas-final-attack-on-israel-and-jewish-people.html.

2. Julia Ioffe and Linda Kinstler, "Now That Russia Has Invaded Ukraine Again, Let's Stop Pretending a Ceasefire Ever Existed," New Republic, November 12, 2014, accessed May 12, 2017, https://newrepublic.com/article/120250/nato-russia-invades-ukraine-breaking-ceasefire-thats-old-news.

3. Marta Kosmyna, "Ukraine Crisis Update: March 18, 2016," Institute for the Study of War, March 18, 2016, accessed May 12, 2017, http://understandingwar.org/backgrounder/ukraine-crisis-update-march-18-2016.

4. Cheryl Chumley, "Iran Threatens 'Strong Slap in the Face' of US," World Net Daily, February 22, 2017, accessed May 12, 2017, http://www.wnd.com/2017/02/iran-threatens-strong-slap-in-the-face-of-u-s/.

5. "North Korea Claims Success in Fifth Nuclear Test," BBC, September 9, 2016, accessed May 12, 2017, http://www.bbc.com/news/world-asia-37314927.

6. "North Korea Propaganda Video Shows Missile Attack Destroying US City," Fox News, April 19, 2017, accessed May

12, 2017, http://www.foxnews.com/world/2017/04/19/north
-korea-propaganda-video-shows-missile-attack-destroying
-us-city.html.

7. "M 7.1—Solomon Islands," United States Geological Survey, January 3, 2010, accessed May 12, 2017, https://earthquake .usgs.gov/earthquakes/eventpage/usp000h5np#executive.

8. "Solomon Islands: Earthquake and Tsunami—Feb 2013," ReliefWeb, accessed May 12, 2017, http://reliefweb.int /disaster/ts-2013-000015-slb.

9. John P. Rafferty and Richard Pallardy, "Chile Earthquake of 2010," *Encyclopædia Britannica*, accessed May 12, 2017, https://www.britannica.com/event/Chile-earthquake-of-2010.

10. "Magnitude 7+ Earthquakes," United States Geological Survey, accessed May 12, 2017, http://tinyurl.com/y7ky9hre.

11. "How Volcano Chaos Unfolded: in Graphics," BBC, accessed May 12, 2017, http://news.bbc.co.uk/2/hi/europe/8634944 .stm.

12. A&E Television Networks, "This Day in History: August 24, 79—Vesuvius Erupts," History.com, accessed May 12, 2017, http://www.history.com/this-day-in-history/vesuvius-erupts.

13. "What's Erupting? List and Map of Currently Active Vol-canoes," VolcanoDiscovery, accessed May 12, 2017, https:// www.volcanodiscovery.com/erupting_volcanoes.html.

14. Somini Sengupta, "Why 20 Million People Are on Brink of Famine in a 'World of Plenty,'" *New York Times*, February 22, 2017, accessed April 6, 2017, https://www.nytimes.com /2017/02/22/world/africa/why-20-million-people-are-on-brink -of-famine-in-a-world-of-plenty.html?_r=0.

CHAPTER 8
COSMIC SIGNS

1. "Comet Shoemaker-Levy Background," NASA, accessed April 6, 2017, http://www2.jpl.nasa.gov/sl9/background.html.

2. Elizabeth Howell, "Shoemaker-Levy 9: Comet's Impact Left Its Mark on Jupiter," Space.com, February 19, 2013, accessed April 6, 2017, http://www.space.com/19855-shoemaker-levy-9 .html.

3. Ibid.

4. Malcolm W. Browne, "Earth-Size Storm and Fireballs Shake Jupiter as a Comet Dies," *New York Times*, July 19, 1994, accessed April 6, 2017, http://www.nytimes.com/1994/07/19 /science/earth-size-storm-and-fireballs-shake-jupiter-as-a -comet-dies.html?pagewanted=all.

5. "Asteroids Ahoy! Jupiter Scar Likely from Rocky Body," NASA Jet Propulsion Laboratory, January 26, 2011, accessed April 6, 2017, https://www.jpl.nasa.gov/news/news.php?release =2011-028.

6. Robert Sanders, "Jupiter Pummeled, Leaving Bruise the Size of the Pacific Ocean," UC Berkeley News, July 21, 2009, accessed April 6, 2017, http://www.berkeley.edu/news/media /releases/2009/07/21_bruise.shtml.

7. Kunio M. Sayanagi, "Jupiter Hit by Another Impactor Thursday; Video Inside," Ars Technica, June 4, 2010, accessed April 6, 2017, https://arstechnica.com/science/2010/06 /breaking-news-jupiter-hit-by-yet-another-impactor/.

8. "Jupiter Impact of Sept. 10, 2012," Space.com, September 11, 2012, accessed April 6, 2017, http://www.space.com/17543 -jupiter-impact-explosion-pictures-amateur-astronomers. html.

9. "Progress Towards the Sustainable Development Goals: Report of the Secretary-General," United Nations, June 3, 2016, accessed April 6, 2017, http://www.un.org/ga/search /view_doc.asp?symbol=E/2016/75&Lang=E.

10. Don Yeomans, Paul Chodas, and Steve Chesley, "Small Asteroid 2009 VA Whizzes By the Earth," NASA Center for Near Earth Object Studies, November 9, 2009, accessed April 6, 2017, http://neo.jpl.nasa.gov/news/news166.html.

11. "Asteroid 2013: DA14 Buzzes, Misses Earth—Unlike Meteor," ABC 15 Arizona, February 15, 2013, accessed April 6, 2017, http://www.abc15.com/news/science-tech/asteroid-2013-da14 -buzzes-misses-earth-unlike-meteor.

12. "Small Asteroid to Safely Pass Close to Earth Sunday," NASA Jet Propulsion Laboratory, September 3, 2014, updated September 12, 2014, accessed April 6, 2017, https://www.jpl.nasa .gov/news/news.php?release=2014-295.

13. Jon Giorgini et al., "Predicting Apophis' Earth Encounters in 2029 and 2036," NASA Center for Near Earth Object Studies,

updated April 16, 2013, accessed April 6, 2017, http://neo.jpl
.nasa.gov/apophis/.

14. Karen C. Fox, "Impacts of Strong Solar Flares," NASA, May
13, 2013, accessed April 6, 2017, https://www.nasa.gov
/mission_pages/sunearth/news/flare-impacts.html.

15. Lynn Cominsky, "Gamma-Ray Bursts: Nature's Brightest
Flash Bulbs," NASA Science, October 21, 2015, accessed April
6, 2017, https://science.nasa.gov/blogs/international-year-light
-blogs/2015/10/21/october-21-2015-gamma-ray-bursts-natures
-brightest-flash-bulbs-lynn-cominsky.

Chapter 9
False Signs and Wonders

1. Mark Cartwright, "Chichen Itza," *Ancient History Encyclopedia*, September 26, 2014, accessed April 7, 2017, http://
www.ancient.eu/Chichen_Itza/.

2. Natalie Wolchover, "Mayan Light Beam Photo: Message
From Gods, or iPhone Glitch?," Live Science, February 27,
2012, accessed April 7, 2017, http://www.livescience
.com/18692-mayan-light-beam-photo.html.

3. Ibid.

4. Mick West, "Why People are 'Suddenly' Seeing Strange
Beams of Light Around the World—The Reddit Effect,"
Metabunk.org, August 20, 2015, accessed April 7, 2017,
https://www.metabunk.org/why-people-are-suddenly-seeing
-strange-beams-of-light-around-the-world-the-reddit-effect
.t6722/.

5. "Mystery Light Beams Appear in Japan 2012 HD," YouTube
video, 2:03, posted by "ADGUKTV," April 11, 2013, accessed
May 12, 2017, https://www.youtube.com/watch?v
=d3WcKMzvoKo.

6. Jordan Breindel, "Heavy Rains in China Create a Magical
Floating City in the Clouds," Taste of Country Network, June
21, 2011, accessed April 10, 2017, http://knue.com/heavy-rains
-in-china-create-a-magical-floating-city-in-the-clouds-video/.

7. "Rare Mirage Appears in Penglai," China Daily, May 8, 2006,
accessed April 10, 2017, http://www.chinadaily.com.cn/photo
/2006-05/08/content_583947.htm.

8. Marc Lallanilla, "Whirling Flames: How Fire Tornadoes Work," Live Science, May 16, 2014, accessed April 10, 2017, http://www.livescience.com/45676-what-is-a-firenado.html.

9. "Very Strange Trumpet Like Sounds Heard Coming From Sky Jan 2016 NEW," YouTube video, 1:58, posted by Real Paranormal Videos, January 18, 2016, accessed April 10, 2017, https://www.youtube.com/watch?v=wht9l4s1QKo.

10. Indigo Nesian, "Strange Weird 'Trumpet' Sounds from the Sky Baffle Residents of Jakarta 09.11.2015," YouTube video, 2:17, September 15, 2015, accessed April 10, 2017, https://www.youtube.com/watch?v=TJ58vMpSy1w.

11. Edmond Tan, ""CMF Trumpet Sounds From Heaven (Warning From God)," YouTube video, 24:16, March 2, 2014, accessed April 10, 2017, https://www.youtube.com/watch?v=IheKrme7yn0.

CHAPTER 10
WITNESSING TO THOSE LIVING AFTER THE RAPTURE (A LETTER IN A BOTTLE)

1. Chas Anderson, "Rapture Print," Armageddon Books, accessed April 10, 2017, http://www.armageddonbooks.com/print.html.

CHAPTER 11
THE BEGINNING OF THE END

1. Guy Edward Farquhar Chilver, "Domitian," *Encyclopædia Britannica*, accessed April 11, 2017, https://www.britannica.com/biography/Domitian.

2. Dan Graves, "In Hoc Signo Vinces [In This Sign Conquer]," Christian History Institute, accessed April 12, 2017, https://www.christianhistoryinstitute.org/incontext/article/constantines-cross/.

3. Constantine, "Edict of Milan," viewed online through Fordham University Internet Medieval Sourcebook, accessed April 12, 2017, http://sourcebooks.fordham.edu/halsall/source/edict-milan.asp.

4. Bible Hub, "Revelation 2:28," accessed May 8, 2017, http://biblehub.com/commentaries/revelation/2-28.htm.

CHAPTER 12
THE FINAL AGES OF THE CHURCH

1. Lyle W. Dorsett, *Billy Sunday and the Redemption of Urban America* (Grand Rapids, MI: Wm. B. Eerdmans, 1991).
2. "Billy Sunday," *New World Encyclopedia*, accessed April 13, 2017, http://www.newworldencyclopedia.org/p/index. php?title =Billy_Sunday&oldid=996618.
3. Dorsett, *Billy Sunday*.
4. "Billy Sunday," *New World Encyclopedia*.

CHAPTER 13
THE SEVEN SEALS

1. "What Is the Average Cost of a Loaf of Bread?," Reference .com, accessed April 13, 2017, https://www.reference.com /food/average-cost-loaf-bread-f32af82c91411d2.
2. John D. Clare, "Hyperinflation," accessed April 13, 2017, http://www.johndclare.net/Weimar_hyperinflation.htm.
3. "Magnitude 10 Temblor Could Happen: Study," *Japan Times*, December 15, 2012, accessed April 18, 2017, http://www .japantimes.co.jp/news/2012/12/15/national/magnitude-10 -temblor-could-happen-study/#.WPI0Y5ArK3A.
4. Anabel Munoz, "USGS Study Says Massive Earthquake Along San Andreas Fault Is Way Overdue in Grapevine," March 7, 2017, accessed April 18, 2017, http://abc7.com /science/usgs-study-says-major-earthquake-in-grapevine -way-overdue/1789999/.
5. "Ring of Fire," National Geographic Society, accessed April 18, 2017, http://nationalgeographic.org/encyclopedia /ring-fire/.
6. USGS FAQs, "Where Do Earthquakes Occur?," United States Geological Survey, accessed April 18, 2017, https://www2 .usgs.gov/faq/categories/9831/3342.
7. "Supervolcano: The World's Biggest Bang," BBC, September 17, 2014, accessed April 18, 2017, http://www.bbc.co.uk/sn /tvradio/programmes/supervolcano/article2.shtml.
8. "Volcano Ash Turns Asian Eclipse Blood Red," Phys.org, June 16, 2011, accessed April 18, 2017, https://phys.org/news /2011-06-volcano-ash-asian-eclipse-blood.html; David C.

Laine, "Examples of Dust From Volcanic Eruptions Blocking the Sun," Sciencing, accessed April 18, 2017, http://sciencing.com/examples-dust-volcanic-eruptions-blocking-sun-14361.html.

9. USGS FAQs, "How Do Volcanoes Erupt?," United States Geological Survey, accessed April 18, 2017, https://www2.usgs.gov/faq/categories/9819/2729.

10. "How Much Energy in a Hurricane, a Volcano, and an Earthquake?," HowStuffWorks.com, August 29, 2012, accessed April 18, 2017, http://science.howstuffworks.com/environmental/energy/energy-hurricane-volcano-earthquake2.htm.

11. "The Atomic Bombings of Hiroshima and Nagasaki," Atomic Archive.com, accessed April 18, 2017, http://www.atomicarchive.com/Docs/MED/med_chp22.shtml.

12. "A History of Iran's Nuclear Program," Wisconsin Project on Nuclear Arms Control, August 9, 2016, accessed April 18, 2017, http://www.iranwatch.org/our-publications/weapon-program-background-report/history-irans-nuclear-program.

13. Robin B. Wright, ed., *The Iran Primer: Power, Politics, and U.S. Policy* (Washington, DC: United States Institute of Peace Press, 2010), 186.

14. "The Atomic Bombings of Hiroshima and Nagasaki," Atomic Archive.com.

CHAPTER 14
THE SEVEN TRUMPETS

1. "Current Incidents," InciWeb, accessed April 18, 2017, https://inciweb.nwcg.gov/0/.

2. Ross Toro, "Half of US Population Lives in Coastal Areas (Infographic)," Live Science, March 13, 2012, accessed April 18, 2017, http://www.livescience.com/18997-population-coastal-areas-infographic.html.

3. "The Battle for the Coast," World Ocean Review, accessed April 18, 2017, http://worldoceanreview.com/en/wor-1/coasts/living-in-coastal-areas/.

CHAPTER 15
THE ARRIVAL OF THE ANTICHRIST AND THE FALSE PROPHET

1. Rose Eveleth, "Why Did I Implant a Chip in My Hand?," *Popular Science*, May 24, 2016, accessed April 18, 2017, http://www.popsci.com/my-boring-cyborg-implant.

ABOUT THE AUTHOR

DOC MARQUIS WAS raised in the Order of the Illuminati and was a Luciferian witch until he got saved on April 15, 1979. He has been fighting against the Illuminati and their plans for a New World Order for the past thirty-eight years. As a result he has produced the following DVDs:

DVD Series: The Secrets of the Illuminati

1. *Arrival of the Antichrist* (2010)

2. *America's Occult Holidays* (2010)

3. *Frontmen of the Illuminati* (2010)

4. *Magick, Mysticism and Masonry* (2010)

5. *Protocols of Zion* (2010)

6. *The Illuminati Is Fulfilling Bible Prophecy* (2010)

7. *The Illuminati's Plan for 2012 and Beyond* (Volume 1) (2011)

8. *The Illuminati's Plan for 2012 and Beyond* (Volume 2) (2011)

9. *Aliens, Fallen Angels or Antichrist?* (Volume 1) (2012)

10. *Aliens, Fallen Angels or Antichrist?*
    (Volume 2) (2012)

11. *Dark Rites and Rituals at the Bohemian
    Grove* (2013)

12. *False Flag Over Boston* (2013)

13. *Dictators of the Illuminati* (2013)

14. *Illuminati Gods at the Olympic Games*
    (Volume 1) (2014)

15. *Illuminati Gods at the Olympic Games*
    (Volume 2) (2015)

DVD Series: It's in the Bible

- *Which Rapture Are We Waiting For?*

- *How Close Are We?*

- *Catholicism: Which Queen of Heaven?*

- *There Were Giants in the Earth*

For any information about DVDs, speaking appearances, or television/radio interviews, please contact Doc Marquis at (402) 228-9476, www.itsagodthingproductions777.com, or docmarquis777@yahoo.com, or find him on Facebook.

CONNECT WITH US!

CHARISMA HOUSE

(Spiritual Growth)

 Facebook.com/CharismaHouse

 @CharismaHouse

 Instagram.com/CharismaHouse

SILOAM

(Health)

 Pinterest.com/CharismaHouse

MODERN ENGLISH VERSION

(Bible)

www.mevbible.com